OCT 2015

the river

the river

HELEN HUMPHREYS

Principal Photography by Tama Baldwin

ECW Press

Get the eBook free!

Purchase the print edition and receive the eBook
free! For details, go to ecwpress.com/eBook.

LIBRARY AND ARCHIVES CANADA
CATALOGUING IN PUBLICATION

Humphreys, Helen, 1961–, author
The river / written by Helen Humphreys.

Issued in print and electronic formats.
ISBN 978-1-77041-255-2 (bound)
ISBN 978-1-77090-784-3 (pdf)
ISBN 978-1-77090-785-0 (epub)

1. Humphreys, Helen, 1961— —Homes and haunts—
Ontario—Napanee River Region. I. Title.

PS8565.U558R59 2015   C818'.54   C2015-902737-3
C2015-902738-1

Editor for the press: Susan Renouf
Cover and text design: Tania Craan
Printing: Friesens   1   2   3   4   5

Printed and bound in Canada

The publication of *The River* has been generously supported by the Canada Council for the Arts which last year invested
$153 million to bring the arts to Canadians throughout the country, and by the Government of Canada through the Canada
Book Fund. *Nous remercions le Conseil des arts du Canada de son soutien. L'an dernier, le Conseil a investi 153 millions de dollars
pour mettre de l'art dans la vie des Canadiennes et des Canadiens de tout le pays. Ce livre est financé en partie par le gouvernement
du Canada.* We also acknowledge the Ontario Arts Council (OAC), an agency of the Government of Ontario, which last
year funded 1,709 individual artists and 1,078 organizations in 204 communities across Ontario, for a total of $52.1 million,
and the contribution of the Government of Ontario through the Ontario Book Publishing Tax Credit and the Ontario Media
Development Corporation.

For Mary Louise

Table of Contents

INTRODUCTION

How can we know anyone or anything?

That is the question that began this book — a desire to know something, in this case a river, on its own terms. I wanted to try to write about nature as it was, not as I wished it to be, and not as a surface that reflected my own struggles and desires. For one thing, I don't think I am as interesting as the river; for another, if I can attempt to truly learn the little swatch of Depot Creek that I have been observing now for a decade, what will I discover? What will be revealed to me if I don't come to the task with expectations of what I will find?

This book is a mix of observation and fiction, historical fact, natural history, and visual documentation. I have given my attempt to know the river everything I have in my novelist's toolbox. I leave it to you to decide if I have succeeded.

Helen Humphreys
June 4, 2015
Bellrock, Ontario

BEGINNINGS

THE RIVER FLASHES black and shiny, coiling between winter trees. In another few months it will be hidden by rushes and swamp grass, will glide silently through the bog under a shroud of burgeoning green.

On the surface of the river lie leaves and blossoms from the flowers that line the banks. On the bottom are lengths of sodden wood, silty hollows choked with old bottles, tires, the bones of animals, the milky bodies of the fish who sway their murky light through the deepening green song of the river. At dusk these fish become lanterns, breathing the last of the sun through their filmy bodies. When I swim they swim with me, staggered above and below, like planes stacked in their individual altitudes.

Under the water the colours are muted, filtered down to a dirty particulate. On the riverbed are bits of pottery, fragments of plates and bowls. When plucked from the water they have black lines of crackle spidering across their white glaze. They are debris from a fire, thrown into the river as garbage and protected by the water, so that now they have well outlasted the people they once belonged to.

The water obscures shape, hides the true nature of objects. For days I swam over a striped piece of wood, and when I finally dived to retrieve it I found that the stripes were teeth and that it was the jaw of a large animal — horse or cow or deer — the teeth yellow and stumpy, socketed into bone so old it had turned to wood and flaked apart in my hands when it left the water for the air.

The river lies in a fault line. Roughly 170 million years old, it is a channel in the earth and communicates constantly with the land along its banks as it flows northeast to south-west, from its headwaters in the Depot Lakes to the shore of Lake Ontario, just below the town of Napanee. The rock it cleaves is what remains of the Grenville Mountains, a billion-year-old range that once stretched from Canada to Mexico and took millions of years to erode into what is now the Canadian Shield.

The river flows down from the six Depot lakes, through the village of Bellrock and the Cameron Bog — a 5,000-acre marsh that is the hinge between the Canadian Shield to the north and a limestone plain to the south. The river moves out of the bog, through the villages of Petworth, Colebrook, Yarker, Newburgh, and Camden East, before emptying into Lake Ontario below Napanee.

Stars stall above the river in summer, and the rocks that jut out along the edge have a nimbus of water around them. Dark planets held in place by current and eddy.

The river ferries twigs and leaves, living and dead creatures along its 35-mile length. It rises and falls with the seasons and the weather, lifting or stranding debris, so that its riverbanks are constantly changing their shape and composition.

The river is not a river at all where I am. It has been downgraded to a creek, only regaining its status as a river farther downstream, in the middle of the Cameron Bog. It has been renamed a creek because it is now dammed at Second and Third Depot Lake, and the flow is diminished from what it once was, except during spring run-off, when the river takes back its shape, rising to the edge of its old riverbanks and losing all its sounds — gone is the hoarse rattle of it running over rocks. Gone is the surge and spill of its waterfalls.

These were the beginnings I wrote for the book, each one entered with hope and confidence that it was the right direction to take. And then each one abandoned, because the fact of the river makes it impossible to define. The fact of the river is that it moves. It moves itself and all its cargo constantly downstream. Because it moves, it can't be contained, and this means too that it can't be contained with words. It can only be met at a particular moment and described for only that moment.

So, this is what I have done.

ANTHROPOCENE

THE PART OF THE RIVER where I am is Algonquin territory. Farther west it was Chippewa, and farther south it was Mohawk. Once the river was known as the "sacred river," and the waterfall at Yarker was known as the "sacred falls" and was a place where warring nations would meet in peace.

Until very recently the land immediately to the west of Bellrock was called Chippewa, the sign placed along an empty country road that leads to a scattering of houses and a large Catholic church. The sign has now been removed; it was the last piece of physical evidence that the Chippewa once inhabited these fields and copses and perhaps had a harvest camp there. Harvest camps were built to include smaller streams and rivers. The Chippewa would fish and harvest wild rice from the waters in the fall in their birchbark canoes. In spring they planted crops and tapped maple trees, flavouring their food all year with the syrup.

The sign that has been removed was once, I imagine, evidence that there was formerly an encampment nearby and when the people themselves left, due to the encroachment of the settlers, the sign was erected the way streets are named after the orchards that were once there and subdivisions after the animals that used to roam freely in the now-paved fields. What seems more plausible is that the place was always known to the white settlers by the existence of the Chippewa camp and so it retained the name, not as a way of honouring the Chippewa who used to live there, but because everyone in the area knew the place by that name and calling it something else would be confusing for them.

When I called the township to ask why the sign had disappeared, no one could give me an answer. They passed me off to a neighbouring township, who then tried to pass me back to South Frontenac. Someone suggested that perhaps the sign had been stolen. Another person couldn't recall there was ever a place with that name. And yet the sign certainly did exist, for I saw it myself, and the place name "Chippewa" is still there on recent ordnance survey maps.

The area around the Depot Creek/Napanee River seems to have always been an important Native hunting and gathering place. In October 1935 a burial mound and evidence of domestic occupation was discovered on a local

farm. The burial mound dated back to the Late Archaic/
Early Woodland period — 3000 B.C. to 1000 A.D. According
to the small newspaper article about the find, "hundreds of
human skeletons" were found "plow deep." Upon discov-
ery, the mound was plundered and the artifacts within it
were sold at auction. The skeletal remains that had rested
undisturbed there for centuries were loaded onto a wagon
and carted away to be dumped and buried in an undisclosed
mass grave.

The burial mound was on a point of land that reached
out into the Cameron Bog, which at the time would have
been a shallow lake. The burgeoning plant life in the lake
slowly drained the water from it over the next thousand
years until it became the marsh it is today.

My little section of the Depot Creek is part of the
present-day Algonquin land claim, a claim that covers
territory from North Bay to the Ottawa Valley, including Algonquin Park and Parliament Hill. The claim is
8.9 million acres in size and is the largest land claim in
Canada's history. The edges of the claim are defined by

various waterways, and the section of Depot Creek from Bellrock down to Petworth is part of the western boundary of the land claim. At Petworth, the river moves back into Chippewa territory, and where it empties into Lake Ontario at Napanee, it is the territory of the Mohawk.

There is precious little of this Native history in the incomers' record — a photograph of artifacts found along the river by an amateur archaeologist in 1913 — a stanza of a poem written in 1850 about the town of Napanee — the fact that the tree we now know as the "paper" birch was once known as the "canoe" birch. The people who lived beside the river for thousands of years, and whose history was intertwined with that landscape, have been very effectively excluded from its recorded narrative.

NAPANEE (1850)

Where lately the forest in dreariness stood,

Where Shippe-caw's wigwam was found in the wood,

Where naught but the owl broke the silence of night,

I here for a while your attention invite.

The axeman directed his steps to this place;

He cared not for Shippe-caw's title or grace;

But boldly the falling of timber commenced;

His cabin he built, and his garden he fenced.

Bellrock was originally Depot Village, or "The Depot," because it was just that, a depot for logs and farm produce and supplies. The river was named after the village and was Depot River. Later, after the dam at Second Depot Lake was constructed, it became Depot Creek. There is a local rumour that it was originally called the Deep Eau River because it was a river of deep water, and on a map from 1878 it is labelled thus, with First Depot Lake being called Deep Eau Lake as well. But it makes no sense to have a French word next to an English one in this way. If the mapmaker was French, why not use two French words, and if the mapmaker was English, why not call it Deep Water River? It seems more likely that the mapmaker didn't understand that the word was meant to be "Depot" or was making a play on it. The 1878 map is the only one — and there are many maps that follow it through the 19th and 20th centuries — that names the river as the Deep Eau River.

When the river was important to the communities it bordered, it was rendered on maps as large and powerful, as taking up a central position. As industry turned away from the river and towards the roads in the 20th century, the river grows smaller in the illustrations of it, until it becomes a spidery squiggle on the maps of today — barely there, like the lines of crackle on the pieces of crockery I haul from the river.

When the river was a livelihood for the settlers it was important, and when it ceased to earn them money, it became less so.

The river itself, of course, has not changed, but the worth assigned it by human beings continues to fluctuate.

The map I like best from the settlement period is the one that comes from the Frontenac County atlas of 1878. Here the river is huge and powerful, a twisting rope of water that muscles through Bellrock, the roads and buildings that border it looking flimsy and insubstantial in comparison. All the contours of the river are carefully marked, as well as the islands and bays. You can almost see the movement of the water. It is a gesture drawing of the river, with the water shaded in with little wave-like dashes and the shoreline expertly outlined, because

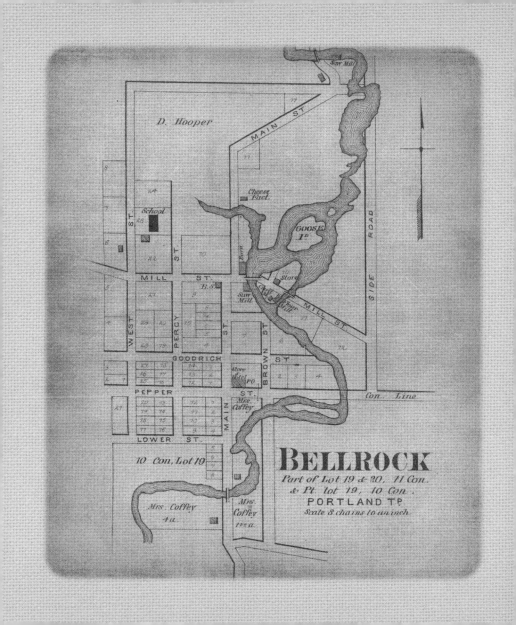

BELLROCK

Part of Lot 19 & 20, 11 Con.
& Pt. lot 19, 10 Con.
PORTLAND TP.
Scale 8 chains to an inch

each narrow and each small harbour meant something, was important to someone. The life in Bellrock at that time centred on the river. In 1878 the village was thriving and boasted a flour mill, cheese factory, sawmill, two stores, one hotel, and a school. There were roads then that aren't here now. There were two blacksmiths in the village, a woolen factor, a carpenter, several merchants, and a Methodist church minister. Bellrock once even had its own independent telephone company, started in 1921 and stopped in 1962, when it was taken over by Bell Canada. All the lines were removed and dismantled by Bell, except for a two-mile section in Bellrock, where the residents refused to relinquish their lines and used the old telephones and line to talk among themselves.

The last vestige of Bellrock's commercial past, the general store, closed in the last 20 years and the mill has long been derelict, although the millrace, overtop of which the wreckage of the mill sits, is still in good order.

Life along the Depot Creek would have remained relatively unchanged for thousands of years until the logging movement in the 19th century, when booms of logs tore the banks of the river, gouging the earth and destroying plant life on the wild ride from the Depot Lakes to the sawmills at Napanee.

The trees were felled in the fall and winter, the logs tied into booms and left on the Depot Lakes until the spring thaw, when they were floated down the chain of lakes and the river using a system of dams and slides to control the volume of water. The harvested trees included maple, basswood, beech, white pine, shagbark hickory, white oak, red oak, white elm, black ash, chestnut oak, red cedar, and hackberry.

The river drivers, mostly French-Canadian, waited out the winter in Bellrock, hunkered down in bunkhouses behind the Bellrock Mill. When spring melted the ice and the river surged into life, these men rode the booms down the winding, bucking length of river to the sawmills. The river drops

200 feet from the Cameron Bog to the town of Napanee, so the spring flow was fast, furious, and dangerous.

There were often over a hundred men on a logging drive, and as a result there were many accidents and drownings on the river during the logging boom. The river drivers made up ballads about the tragedies, and sang them long afterwards, while they worked the logs downstream.

In 1866 the Napanee River Improvement Company was started with a mandate to improve the supply of water on the river for manufacturing purposes, as there were many water-powered saw- and gristmills along its length in the settler days. The company built additional dams which impeded the timber drives and interfered with the sawmills operating at Napanee because the flow of the water wasn't consistent. The new dams also flooded farmland bordering the river and brought the unwelcome wrath of the farmers. During the Napanee River Improvement Company's long tenure, these farmers frequently dynamited or destroyed the dams to stop their lands from being flooded. This was such a common practice that the company offered a thousand-dollar reward for information leading to the conviction of those responsible for "blowing up and otherwise injuring the dams."

No one was ever caught. The reward was never claimed.

Mortimer Meeks, the agent for the Napanee River Improvement Company, who was based in Bellrock, wrote the following letter to D.B. Stickney, president of the company, on April 14, 1890, about a dam in the Depot Lakes chain.

"The only person on the place is Conway's oldest girl. She says she is going to stay there and watch the dam, but I think she will starve out in a few days. And what can she do any way in case the dam is torn open, and there is people near there that would rip the dam open in short order if they was not afraid the company would law them."

There were dams on all the Depot Lakes and many places on the river in 1890.

After a century of cutting down the forests along the Depot Lakes, the last log drive on the river took place in 1905.

The Napanee River Improvement Company kept going for another 57 years, finally stopping operation in 1962.

The Hardwood Creek that cuts through the Cameron Bog to the east of Bellrock was once what its name suggests, a rich stand of maples, oaks, birches, ash, elm, and beech, all harvested by the Rathburn Logging Company, who controlled logging along the Depot Lakes chain in the late 19th century. Before logging, the trees in the area were magnificent giants. A local woman wrote about a white pine whose trunk could only be encircled by three people joining hands around the girth of the tree.

The impressive forests are gone and the banks of Hardwood Creek are now lined with saplings and impenetrable bog willow. The area is now known locally as the Long Swamp or the Drowned Lands, and it is thought that the constant rising and lowering of the water levels caused by the dams helped to create the bog. It was clearly less boggy before logging, as strips of land along the river through what is now the bog were once owned by individuals, and, in settler mentality, there would have been no benefit in owning land that could not be used.

In 1957 the Ontario government was even considering draining a portion of the bog and turning it into a large vegetable-growing area — "truck farming" as they called it then — similar in size and scale to the Holland Marsh north of Toronto.

It is interesting to note that all through the early and mid-20th century, Nature was a proper noun, with a capital N.

In 1878 a Mrs. Coffey owned my two acres of river. Her name is printed on the page of the atlas that shows Bellrock, which meant that she paid to have it there and which also meant that she was, or thought of herself as, someone of importance.

Mary Coffey (sometimes spelled Coffee or Coffy) was born in Ireland in 1821. She was Roman Catholic, and had a daughter named Julia who was reportedly born in Ireland around 1854. It appeared that Mary immigrated to Canada somewhere between 1854 and 1860, as she is listed on the 1861 census in Portland Township. She is described as being a widow, but the interesting thing is that there is no indication that there ever was a Mr. Coffey, either in Canada or back in Ireland.

Was Mary Coffey a single mother who left Ireland, or was made to leave Ireland because she was pregnant? Was Julia even her daughter — although both the 1881 and 1891 census say that she was. Did they come to Canada as a result of the Irish Potato Famine? And did she have her baby in Canada? In 1852 there is a Mary Coffee who is listed as living with a large Catholic family in a neighbouring township, but she is listed as "single" on the census, and there is no mention of her having a child, or of there being a child named Julia.

What is known is that Mary Coffey played a large part in the community of Bellrock. At various times, and sometimes simultaneously, she was the proprietor of the Bellrock Hotel, the village postmistress, and she ran the general store. No other person in the village had so many roles within it.

Oddly, Julia stayed with her mother, never marrying, and while she took over running the general store when Mary died, she followed her mother to the grave. Mary died of "old age" in 1891 at the age of 70, and Julia died three years later of consumption at the age of 40.

The facts of these two lives raise more questions than they answer. If Julia stayed with her mother for her whole life was this because there was something the matter with her and she was unable to cope without care? Or did the likelihood of Mary being a single mother create a special bond between the two women so that they didn't want to be parted? Or did Mary Coffey have a particular hold over her daughter, required her to work for her, and so Julia was never free to live her own life apart from her mother?

Bellrock in the latter part of the 19th century was a rough and largely male society. The river drivers who spent the winter in the village waiting for the ice to melt would have spent that time drinking, gambling, fighting, and whoring. So how was it that the Coffey women felt safe enough to live for almost 30 years in the village by themselves? It could be that "Mrs." Coffey was a commanding presence and ran so much of the village that she was afforded respect and no one dared to cross her. Or it could be that Julia worked as a prostitute in the hotel that her mother ran and this also afforded the two women a relatively safe passage.

Whatever the truth, what is evident from the facts is that Mary Coffey was a good businesswoman, and that she left this world with considerably more than she had when she entered it. And although she clearly operated everything herself, when she died she was listed in the obituary as a "merchant's wife" when she was, in fact, the merchant.

What was once the Coffey house, a small frame building of a storey and a half, sits about 30 feet distant from the river. The owner before me put in two large sliding glass doors to cover the wall that faces the water because there had been no windows there, no glimpse of the beautiful river view. But in Mary Coffey's time the river would have been a very public place, with the river drivers shouting and cursing as they rode the log booms downstream, and the booms crashing against the rocks and the riverbanks. If there had been windows on the side of the house that faced the river, then there would have been no privacy from the river, and privacy would have been desirable then and much more important than the view of the water that I am so attached to now.

The National Hotel burned down in the late 19th century, and the pieces of charred china that I sometimes pull from the river would likely have been from that fire. The hotel was across the road from the river and from Mary Coffey's little frame house, and it would have made sense to throw the debris from the fire into the river. The water feels like a sort

of moving darkness, capable of hiding and taking everything away without consequence.

Depot Village became Bellrock in 1861. There are many explanations for the new name. It is said that the village was named after the owner of the first sawmill, a James Bell (although this doesn't explain the "rock" part of the name). It is said that the rocks in the area are shaped like the tops of bells, and this is how the village got its moniker. On the old maps it is spelled both as one word, "Bellrock," and as two, "Bell Rock." I wondered briefly if there actually was a bell rock in the area, a rock that, when struck, made a loud clanging sound like a bell and was used by various Native tribes to summon their members. There is an example of a bell rock in the Cloche Mountains near Georgian Bay, and as this land is similar in geological make-up to the eroded Grenville range in eastern Ontario, it is possible that a bell rock could exist here. But I doubt that, if there had been one of these magical sites near the village, the settlers would have wanted to memorialize it. As with the Chippewa encampment, the interest was in erasing the Native presence in the area, not remembering it.

One of the descendants of the family that lived on my property for much of the 20th century wrote me that she had been told the village was called Belle Roque by the French river drivers who spent the winters there. Belle Roque — Good Rest — makes a lot of sense, as the river drivers were indeed resting until the spring thaw. And if that is the true meaning of the village name, then it is interesting to note that the French roots of Bellrock have also been largely forgotten.

When the river was dammed at Second Depot Lake in 1947, the log booms no longer careened downriver to the sawmills, but livelihoods were still made from the river. The Bellrock mill continued to operate as a gristmill and made cheese boxes for local cheese factories, employing several people from the village.

In the early part of the 20th century, Russell Revelle and his family lived in the little frame house on my property. Russell was a frogger, catching bullfrogs on the river in summer and selling the frog legs to restaurants in Montreal and Toronto. In winter he trapped and, apparently, had traplines all over Frontenac County. His daughter, Dorothy, remembered his skill at maneuvering his canoe along the river, and how he paddled so expertly that he never lifted the paddle blade out of the water.

Russell's son took over the family business of trapping and frogging. His great-nieces remember seeing 50-pound burlap potato sacks writhing with live frogs on the riverbanks. He kept the sacks wetted down until he was ready to kill the frogs and freeze the legs in preparation for transport to the restaurants.

Bullfrogs apparently are attracted to the colour red and a rather genteel way of catching them used to be to spread a red tablecloth on the bank of a river. The frogs would simply hop onto the cloth, as though you were inviting them to a picnic. But the method favoured by most froggers, and probably used by Russell and his son, was to "jack" the frogs by shining a light into their eyes at night, immobilizing them with panic and confusion, and making it easy to grab them.

Bullfrog populations have been severely depleted from being eaten, but even so, they are not considered a species at risk and are not currently protected by conservation laws.

There are few bullfrogs on my little stretch of river, so few that I always take note when I hear or see them. This summer I didn't hear or see a single one.

The Revelles

The river changes volume constantly. In spring it swells back to its original banks, and at the end of August it rattles with emptiness. When the river is wide and fast there are no rocks showing below the surface and it is a racing, flexing sinew, where the speed of the current can be seen on the surface of the water. When it is high and fast, when it is full of itself, it makes less noise. It fills its voice.

How to fit to the rhythm of something whose rhythms keep changing?

The river flows through winter, never freezing at the little waterfall. In winter the water looks black against the snow and the surge over the waterfall often carries bits of ice to the little bay below the falls. Once, I saw otters playing in the waterfall on a winter's day and I have sometimes found their tracks in the snow around the cabin.

In an especially cold winter the bay below the waterfall will freeze and the water that bubbles over the falls will slide under a shelf of ice there and disappear. I have always felt that this makes the ice fundamentally unstable and so have never attempted to walk upon it. Two owners before me, the woman who lived here had her dog fall through this ice and drown.

When the water level drops, the river is noisier and the noise is something to lean into. It becomes the loudest noise in the immediate environment and can be heard from everywhere on the two-acre property.

When the river is lower it also seems faster because the movement is visible — where it breaks over rocks or dekes around them. The low water and the high rocks make the water churn white where it passes over the rocks, and having this second colour in the water also makes the movement more pronounced and makes the flow seem faster. It feels and sounds like an argument, whereas the high and silent river seems like a decision.

The movement of the water around the rocks looks like the water is climbing itself; the backwards curl of white as the waterfall surges forward and a fold of water arches over looks like batter being folded in a bowl.

WHAT
THE RIVER
HAS BROUGHT
ME OVER
THE YEARS

- three chairs — two wooden Adirondack chairs, and one aluminum lawn chair with yellow plastic webbing
- two clay smoking pipes from the 1800s, manufactured in Scotland and with the name of the manufacturer — McDougall — still visible
- a green-and-white-swirled child's marble
- the jawbone of a cow or deer
- many broken plates, bottles, and cups
- old pop and medicine bottles
- a ceramic doorknob
- a pair of pliers
- an inflatable dinghy
- a fishing net
- a fishing rod
- a beachball
- a wicker basket

- plastic minnow pails
- a shovel
- a rubber tire
- a wooden trellis
- a small plastic cow from a child's farm set
- a headless sheep in a burlap sack
- a 16-foot motorboat without the motor

CATTAIL

THE CABIN IS DARK in the early morning. The windows are small, set high in the log walls, and when the light fumbles through them it falls only on the large objects in the room

— the trestle table, the loom, the corner cupboard. She can never see well enough, and this is how she burned her hand this morning, because the mouth of the fireplace was a shadowy cave and as she knelt to light the fire, she couldn't tell that yesterday's fire still smoldered in the grate.

Accidents happen more often than she cares to admit. She blames it on the windows, but she could just as easily blame it on the new life, this new life that means living in this small cabin in a clearing hacked out of the surrounding forest. But she doesn't blame the new life. Instead she wrenches open the door of the corner cupboard and feels around for the tin of salve to rub on her burned hand. Then she goes back to building up the fire so that there will be heat in the brick oven cut into the wall. She will put the bread in to bake there when the fire is hot enough, and then set about the tasks of the day. There are two main tasks today — to stuff a mattress, and to finish weaving a large basket that she intends to use for carrying in the vegetables from the garden plot out back of the cabin. Later, she will boil a pot of water and make a stew for supper. Then, when the sun has set behind the trees, she will go outside and light the torches to place on the path in front of the cabin, so that if it is tonight that her husband returns from hunting, he will be able to find his way back to her.

The old life included dances and teas, carriage rides through the park. In the new life there are sometimes clouds of flies so thick that after she battles her way through them blood drips down her neck from the chunks of flesh they've chewed out of her head. In the old life she could buy oranges and chocolate, yards of taffeta for a fancy dress. In the new life the deer eat most of her vegetables and she crawls through the garden at the end of September, scratching out the last of the potatoes from the thick, clinging soil. In the new life she wears the same frayed cotton shift day after day — the hem burned from standing too close to the fire, the bodice stained with sweat.

What is it then? What keeps her here? It's not love, although she does love her husband and followed him willingly when he journeyed to this country with the promise of free land. It's not duty. It's not the spirit of adventure because, quite frankly, after the third trek through the boggy backcountry, that wears off.

When she was young she would lie in her bed and watch the birds outside her window, how they lifted and fell in the sky with the rhythm of her breath. She would run with the hunting dogs through the stubbled fields, feeling the stretch and pull of their hunger as they chased a rabbit down.

This is how she has desired to live, this feeling of being used up utterly, of there being nothing left over at the end of a day, at the end of her life. In the old world there was always a

holding back because there could be, because there was safety there. In this new place she can spend herself completely. The landscape is a mirror for her desires. Today she has used only the cattail. She has used the fibres to stuff a mattress, the dry leaves to weave a basket. She has baked bread with flour ground from the cattail head, and she will cook the base of the plant tonight in her stew, to substitute for potatoes. When she burned her hand, the salve she used to calm the wound was made from the mashed up roots of the cattail. And tonight, the torches that she will set in the ground outside the cabin to guide her husband home will be the lit heads of the marsh plant. She has used everything. There will be nothing left over. And in this act she feels great satisfaction because she knows, to the end of herself she knows, that this is how she was meant to live.

I THOUGHT THE VOYAGE OVER would be the worst. We had been warned about the number of dead on board the ships, how these *coffin ships* left Ireland with a roster of healthy travellers and arrived in Montreal carrying a cargo of dead passengers. We had been warned, but we came anyway, because facing possible death was still better than facing the certain death of the famine.

We carried the few possessions that we couldn't be parted from, or that might be worth something if we needed to sell them on arrival in the New World. We also brought with us whatever food we could scrounge before we left, mostly cabbages and turnip greens because these would keep better than anything else on the long journey over the Atlantic.

Table No 4

Hospital Report of the Detachment of the 32ᵈ Regiment stationed at Grosse-Isle from April 30th to October 31st inclusive 1834

Diseases	Cholera	Fev Cont C	Fev Typh	Pleuritis	Pneumonia	Total
Admitted	6	3	7	1	1	18
Discharged	4	3	3	1	1	12
Died	2	.	4	.	.	6

Nominal list of those who have died.

		Admitted	Died	
William Slack	Fev Typh	June 5th	June 12th	Hospital nurse
Patk McDonough	"	" 21	July 2ᵈ	
John Morgan	"	" 22	" 11	
John Cahill	Cholera	Augt 2	Augt 9	Attacked with Cholera while in the Fever Ward & died same day
Thos Greenwood	Cholera	" 10	" 11	
Wm Shall	"	" 22ᵈ	" 22	Telegraph Order by passing thro' the Sheds daily

Chas Poole M.D.
Med. Supt.

I thought we were doing well, my husband and I. We had spent the crossing on deck whenever possible, away from the fevers of the hold, and we still had two cabbages left in our burlap sack when our ship entered the St. Lawrence River.

No one had mentioned the quarantine. But here we were, not in Montreal, as we had anticipated, but on an island in the middle of the river, an island with a French name and fitted out with quarantine hospitals where we were expected to remain, with the passengers who had already contracted typhus, until we either became ill ourselves or stayed well.

"Could you not just take those who are ill?" my husband asked one of the officers, as we stood at the ship's rail and waited our turn to disembark. "We have kept to ourselves on the voyage so that we would not catch the fever."

"Everyone goes into quarantine," said the officer. "There are no exceptions."

But when we walked off the boat onto the island, we were told that the hospitals were filled to capacity, and that we were being moved to the fever sheds on Windmill Point. And here, because we were housed so closely together with passengers who were ill, my husband caught the fever.

The nurses who attended the fever sheds were French nuns. They wore grey cloaks and I could not understand anything they said to us. Just as we had done on board the ship, we kept to ourselves. I sat with my husband in a corner of our fever shed and I tried to avoid getting too near the other patients as I mopped Cathal's brow with a rag I had torn from the hem of my skirts.

I ate one of the cabbages, chewing the leaves slowly to fool my belly into thinking that I had eaten a full meal.

Cathal died at night. The nuns had placed more candles around the very ill, so they knew who to tend first, and the glow from the candles hid the evidence of my husband's illness — the sweating and faraway eyes — but showed up the movement of his body as he struggled for breath. I sat at the end of his cot and watched as his chest rose and fell. His body was thin and the shape of his ribs heaving up and down in the candlelight looked strangely like the wings of a butterfly, opening and closing, preparing for flight. It felt cruel to me to be given so beautiful an image for my husband's dying.

I was not allowed to keep the body. They buried Cathal in a mass grave with no marker. There were so many dead that they could not keep up with the burials. They just pushed the bodies into an open pit and when the pit was full, dirt was shovelled on top of the corpses.

When I was past caring whether I died or not, the nuns declared me free from typhus and I was sent on to Montreal. I arrived at the docks with a silver locket and two gold coins sewn into the bodice of my dress, and the burlap sack with the remaining cabbage in my hands. I had no appetite from grief and had not eaten the second cabbage, but I knew better than to part with it.

The docks were swarming with other travellers, some so thin from the weeks of starving in quarantine that they could barely walk down the gangplank. I moved away from the docks as quickly as I could, away from my fellow countrymen, from the memory of that terrible crossing. I moved onto the streets of Montreal, another poor Irish immigrant, alone in a city whose language I could not speak.

To stay alive I would need to find work and shelter, and both of these tasks seemed impossible to imagine at the moment. I sat down on the earth between two buildings, away from the scorch of the sun. The earth was cool to the touch, like water.

I took the last cabbage from the sack and peeled off the rotting outer leaves. There, nestled in the inner leaves of the cabbage was a gauzy pouch where a worm had made a shroud of itself and was waiting to become a butterfly. It seemed almost miraculous that such a tiny creature had accompanied us on the voyage from Ireland, had survived on the food we had brought for ourselves, and now was transforming itself before my eyes. It suddenly became of the greatest importance that this tiny creature continue to live. It was as though our fates

were joined, and if the butterfly broke through the shroud and flew off into the summer air, then I too would be able to survive the transformation from the old world to the new one.

It took two full days for this change to happen. In those days I remained crouched between the two buildings. I ate the cabbage around where the worm had nested, and on the third day it broke through the shroud. It was a small, white butterfly, such as I had seen on the cabbages at home. It opened and closed its new wings, trying them out, and it was hard in that moment not to believe that the butterfly had been sent by my husband, and that its flight was a message of hope.

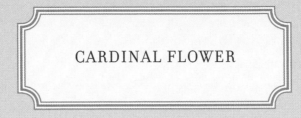

CARDINAL FLOWER

1620

H E KNEELS BY the streambed. The light drifts through the trees like smoke. It is late afternoon, and he has been here since early morning. Tomorrow the expedition ship sails back to France and he will have this plant on board as a specimen, but today he is visiting it where it grows along the banks of this woodland stream.

The red of the blade-like petals is so intense it takes his breath away. The red is as bright as sudden feeling, or the song of the lark. It is as bright as blood — arterial blood, not the blue venous hum. The red is arterial blood with a velvet plushness behind it.

That's it, he thinks. *The flower colour is as rich as the robes of the Roman Catholic cardinals.*

It is the end of summer. The red flowers threaded along the edge of the stream are dying. The petals near the base of the plant are withered and dry, their colour gone. The botanist crouches in the soft grass, inspecting the underside of the flower. It dies the way darkness arrives — from the ground up. Soon only the topmast of the plant will be alive, lighting the water's edge like a torch.

Beside the flower, on the ground by the botanist's feet, is the burlap bag he will fill with the plant and some earth from the streambank. Once inside the bag, the flame of the flower will be extinguished, and the botanist delays the moment of uprooting. He can feel in that moment something of his own ending — the flicker of his own pulse, darkening.

William Bligh takes the lid from the wooden barrel. The red of the flower never ceases to astonish him every time he comes amidships. He feels winded, holding the wooden barrel lid with one hand and putting the other hand up to his heart.

Lid on. Lid off. He can't decide. For three days he left the cardinal flower in full sun and it seemed to thrive, but on the fourth day it wilted and he has kept it covered ever since. But now the colour seems a little blanched and he thinks it might be time to leave the flower under the open skies again.

This fickleness delights him, although he would never admit this, even to himself. *Capricious*, that's the word that came to him in the middle of last night, that woke him as thoroughly as if he'd been splashed with cold water. This certainty of colour is equally balanced by a whimsical temperament.

William Bligh is not capricious. He is steady, dependable. This is why he's been appointed as Master to James Cook's ship, *Resolution*. He is good — no, skilled — at making charts and at navigation. He is reliable and thorough.

I am boring, he thinks, looking into the blush of the cardinal flower. *I am boring, and the men loathe me.*

They are sailing back to England. The voyage has been curtailed with Cook's unexpected death in Hawaii after he rather unwisely provoked an armed conflict with the natives there. Bligh is in temporary command of the ship and, in the absence of Cook, he is trying to keep some of the dead explorer's spirit on board by keeping to the same routines that Cook insisted upon on the voyage out. The crew must be kept clean and

healthy. To this end they are to have regular baths and fresh clothing. They are to eat sauerkraut and drink lime juice for protection against scurvy. And they are to have mandatory dancing every day from 5:00 in the evening until 8:00 at night.

It is the dancing that is causing the most trouble. Three hours of enforced dancing a day with one's fellow sailors is not bringing out the best in anyone. Several of the men have pretended to come down with scurvy in order to avoid the dancing, forgetting perhaps that their diet (which they also complain about) makes it impossible for them to have actually contracted the disease. But it is increasingly tedious having to deal with the resistance, and the complaints.

"I am only trying to do what's good for them," says William Bligh to the cardinal flower. He feels foolish, having said this out loud, looks around to see if anyone has heard him.

There are a multitude of barrels on the deck of the *Resolution*. Each barrel has holes punched in the sides. Each one is filled with soil, and each contains a plant. Some of the plants, like the cardinal flower, were taken from the earliest portion of the journey, from the shores of North America. Quite a few of these specimens have not survived. The plants found in the West Indies have been on board for far less time, and these are thriving. Perhaps the roll of the ship unsettles the specimens. They are used to the unmovable earth. Perhaps the roll of the ship makes their roots clutch desperately to the little patch of soil in the barrels, and this takes all their energy. William Bligh ponders this, head bent over the cardinal flower as though in prayer. He hopes that this flower is too bright to die, that it could be as simple as that. He has come to depend on the visit every day, this moment when he stands before the barrel and sees that start of red.

The light is heavier in the sky. The hour of dancing is almost upon them. William Bligh lays the barrel lid carefully on the deck. He takes one last look at the crimson flower, sighs, plucks his watch from his breast pocket to confirm the time.

It is as he feared.

When I have my own ship, he thinks as he walks astern. *When I have my own ship, things will be different.*

1827

The apothecary lies at the base of the willow tree. He is curled into a sweating ball, hands clutching at his guts. It feels as though there are hot snakes crawling through him. Each spasm makes his body jolt, causes a small anguished moan to escape his lips. Each moment is worse than the moment before, and it seems that this torture can only, will only, end in his death. The pain is so severe that he would welcome death at this point.

Perhaps he had become overconfident in his success with *bittersweet*. He had watched intently as his Indian guide had crushed the berries and mixed them with bear grease. He hadn't needed the translator to explain that the paste could be rubbed on the skin to cure bruising. He had tried it himself, combining the juice of the *bittersweet* berries with bacon fat and slathering it over the bruises on his knees, from when he'd tumbled down that cliff face trying to get to a nest of gull's eggs. The berry juice must have powerful properties that dissolved congealed blood, for his bruises disappeared overnight.

It had seemed simple enough. The guide had pointed to where the cardinal flower attached to the earth, had mimed the drinking of tea, had rubbed his stomach. Surely this could only mean that the apothecary boil the roots into a tea that would cure stomach complaints? He didn't need a translator to tell him that. In fact, the apothecary had decided he didn't need the translator at all, had sent him back to his village. Why continue to pay for a service he didn't require? What a waste of good money.

The pain rocks him, and he tries to curl tighter against it, tries to shut it out.

The apothecary had been very excited about the cardinal flower tea. He had heard tell from other herbalists that it could be the cure for many ailments — epilepsy, syphilis, typhoid, stomach aches, worms. Now, as he rolls around on the streambank under the willow tree, it seems to him that instead of curing those complaints, the tea has given them to him. He looks out at the bright splashes of flowers along the edge of the water, and he suddenly feels cold with fear. What if he got it wrong? What if the guide wasn't rubbing his stomach to extol the virtues of the tea, but to warn him against drinking the brew?

The apothecary closes his eyes. Ever since he knew the value of it, people have accused him of being mean with money, and now it seems this meanness is to cost him his life.

1857

John Gould hides behind the screen of alders. He has been waiting for what seems like hours, but is, in reality, only a matter of minutes.

John Gould is an industrious man. He is not used to waiting, prefers to be doing. In 1857, still only in his early fifties, he has produced over two thousand colour lithographs of birds, some of them illustrating a particular bird for the first time. He has also had his own taxidermy business since he was a boy, thus providing himself with the specimens to be drawn. It is a remarkable output, but although the bird pictures are attributed to him, and he does nothing to dissuade this, it isn't really John Gould who creates them. He has friends and employees who do the work, including the lyricist Edward Lear and John's own wife, Elizabeth. In fact, Elizabeth was his chief illustrator for years, until she died in childbirth in 1841 at the age of 37. It was really Elizabeth who was the prolific one — all those colour plates, and six living children. John is merely a good businessman, but Elizabeth had the talent.

The bird that excites John Gould's passions like no other is the hummingbird. He has collected thousands of stuffed specimens, which have been recently displayed to great acclaim at the Regent's Park Zoological Gardens. Even Queen Victoria is said to have become enchanted by his hummingbirds.

Hummingbirds were once thought to be small flying fires. The Aztec rulers prized their coloured feathers and wore robes made entirely from their skins. It is thought that, because of the popularity of Gould's hummingbird exhibition,

these robes might come back in fashion, this time among the British aristocracy. It takes thousands of skins to make a single garment, and John Gould is not in favour of this degree of carnage sweeping through the ranks of his beloved humming-birds. He feels guilty for inspiring it, and this is partly why he is here, in North America, crouched behind this screen of alders at the bank of this stream. In all his years of collecting hummingbirds, he has yet to see a live one, and he desperately wants to see one before he dies, or before the birds have been sacrificed to the whims of fashion.

Along the bank of the stream grows the brilliantly coloured cardinal flower. This flower is the favourite of the ruby-throated hummingbird, and John Gould hopes to see the tiny bird at dusk when it comes to visit the flowers.

The cardinal flower is the richest red Gould has ever seen in nature. It makes sense to him that the hummingbird would be attracted to something even more beautiful than itself. *We all want to serve a higher being*, he thinks, and he remembers Elizabeth, hunched over her drawings, a halo of candlelight stuttering around her head. *No*, he thinks. *We all want to possess a higher being*, and he looks down at the small gauzy cage that hangs from a piece of whalebone attached to a button on his vest. John Gould doesn't just want to observe the humming-bird. He wants to catch one. It will live inside this little bag of gauze. He has worked out how to feed it through the mesh with a small, slender-necked bottle. The bird will be a quick flash of red, like this woodland flower. The bird will flutter and whirr on the outside of his body, just above his heart.

MORPHOLOGY

A STRAIGHT RIVER is either very young or very old. This river is full of curves at its headwaters, but straightens out the farther south it goes, as the sheer velocity of water on its way to Lake Ontario takes a direct path, doesn't have the time to deviate around peninsulas or bays.

Sometimes when the river floods in spring and the water is moving quickly up here at the headwaters, the river tries to cut off the curves and carves a straight line across the grass. Speed isn't charitable. At a certain momentum, the river becomes all about getting there.

This spring the river was deeper than I ever remember, high and cold and running with a strong current. When it is high like this, I can hear the push of the water over the waterfall, the exact sound of the surge. I can't hear this when the water is low because then what I hear is the water over the rocks and shallows. I wonder if there is a volume that the river prefers, a volume when it feels more like itself? Because it has been dammed and used to run higher and with greater force, does it feel more like itself when it is high and deep and running fast? When the river is shallow, does it feel starved?

When the river is low, the structure of the bottom becomes visible and difficult to navigate. When the river is high, it's all surface and there is an ease to moving along on the surface without having to consider what lies beneath.

In the winter the margins of the river shrink due to ice build-up at the edge of the riverbanks. In the summer the margins shrink because of the waterlilies and bog willows that crowd the edge of the river. So, only in the spring and fall (and more so the spring) is the river unencumbered by what it supports and promotes within its boundaries.

In July there is weed growth in the river; the weeds lying down like slimy mermaid hair in the current and slime coating all the rocks. In August the weeds are gone and with the bright sun overhead, it is possible to see right down to the riverbed in places. All my diving and recovery of artifacts has been done in this August light.

It takes roughly four hours to canoe from Bellrock to Yarker, where the journey must end because of the large waterfall there, and the series of swifts and rapids that lie beyond the falls.

The first part of the voyage, down Depot Creek to the bridge over the Long Swamp Road and then under that bridge and onto the Napanee River proper all the way down to Petworth, is arguably the best part of the journey. This portion is entirely through the bog and so there is no human habitation, just a couple of rotting wooden duck blinds from decades ago. The river is only navigable by canoe and because the first part of the river requires hauling out over several beaver dams, it does not seem to be very much used by canoeists.

In a decade, I have only ever met one other canoe on this first stretch of the river. The lack of human habitation and the utter remoteness of the bog make it seem timeless. The animal life along the river is unused to a human presence and is relatively easy to spot. I have seen deer sleeping in their beds along the riverbanks in the early morning, and owls lifting and lowering on huge and silent wings through the trees. The drowned lands are home to a substantial heronry, and the beavers are so unruffled by the occasional human being that they swim right under the canoe, not bothering to warn other beavers of danger with their customary tail slap on the water.

One of the old Depot Creek stories is of a farmer who had sheared his sheep and left the pile of fleeces in the yard while he went into the farmhouse for lunch. A swirling wind blew the fleeces into the air, towards the swamp, where they lodged in trees and the crows used them as nests for years afterwards.

The bog trees that haven't been drowned are largely maple and ash. Bog willow and pussywillow grow in profusion along the banks, as do marsh plants such as arrowhead, cardinal flower, yarrow, pickerelweed, loosestrife, and marsh marigold. There are carpets of ferns in the woods.

Just before Petworth, when it is necessary to line the canoe through the rapids there, the riverbed changes from loose granite rocks to smooth sheets of limestone as the geological landscape shifts from Canadian Shield to the Napanee limestone plain. It happens suddenly, with no gradations. One moment, you are canoeing over a dark tumble of stones, and the next there is a grey wash of limestone beneath the boat. The water lightens accordingly. When the riverbed was Canadian Shield, when it was composed of the insides of the old Grenville Mountain range, the granite was black from the sediment and organisms in the water. Again, it seems a sort of moving dark. But the limestone bed as refracted through the water is much brighter and lighter in hue and the water becomes a light tobacco colour with the bottom of the riverbed visible for most of the remainder of the canoe down to Yarker.

The rust- or tobacco-coloured water of the river is caused, at its headwaters, by the mineral content of the Precambrian shield. When one enters the limestone plain at Petworth, the tobacco colour is now caused by the particulate from the Cameron Bog.

Objects floating on top of the water are reflected under the water, but the shapes are distorted by the water itself — an elm leaf looks like a clover leaf, and a tiny stick looks bulbous and segmented, like a bloated worm. Something submerged is reflected through a watery prism and appears as a shadow on the rocks and river bottom, on what is beneath the water.

Water striders are a shifting constellation
on the dark, moving surface of the river.

A leaf moves downstream
at the rate of 0.3 miles per hour.

The shore vegetation works against the river, crowding in, trying to take over the space held by the water — but the current and the volume and the power of the water keeps the vegetation at bay. When a river dries up, the shoreline vegetation takes over very quickly.

What moves quickest takes precedence — the water is swifter than the growth of the vegetation at its banks, so the water, or the movement of the water, is able to keep back the movement of the growing vegetation.

Once, at a time when the river was flooded in spring, I saw a snake being borne away by the current, twisting and thrashing as the river pulled it downstream. It looked so helpless, and yet movement usually worked for the snake. It had simply come up against something with a greater capacity for movement. Another example of how what is swiftest has dominion.

The river always carries the scent of rain. At night the smell, the cool tang of it, rises up to fill the night, where in daylight the river hides its scent or the sunlight neutralizes it. Water and darkness are aligned.

The smell of the bog is part of the river, and the bog is responsible for its colour. In the strong spring run-off you can really smell it as the river churns its way downstream to Napanee. The water surges over the falls at Yarker like a wild animal springing forward, hanging on its leash of quieter water upstream — frothy and violent and exciting. When I visited a house built over the falls at Yarker, the river was so noisy that it could be heard indoors, when the windows were closed. The sound and sight of the water's movement over the falls would never be anything less than intense, and I wonder how the sheer force and power of the river there changes or affects the thoughts and feelings of the humans who live in such close proximity to it. There is a multitude of scientific proof that waterfalls fill the air around them with negative ions, and these negative ions lift the mood, energy, and health of human beings. The more turbulent the waterfall, the more negative ions it produces. Those who live near, or next to, a waterfall, are inclined to be less depressed, have fewer migraines, and possess more energy than people who live in an urban environment.

The river sounds like applause when it's low and making noise over the stones on its way downstream.

It sings in a contralto voice and the deeper it is, the quieter it gets. The waterfall itself is in the key of A, which is also the key to which an orchestra tunes when they are warming up.

When the wind blows opposite to the flow of the river, the ripples on its surface make it look as though the current is going north. This makes it seem as if the river would disappear into a landscape where one couldn't follow, rather than flowing south and taking us towards the towns and cities that exist there. Flowing south is the easier direction for us, the tamer way. North would take the river from what we know to what is out of reach.

From the mid-1800s a mysterious tide has been observed at the Napanee River mouth. Objects have been seen floating downstream, only to return upstream in a few hours' time. The phenomenon is called a "seiche" effect and is the result of the prevailing southwesterly winds on Lake Ontario pushing water to the north shore of the lake. When the winds subside, the water flows back out towards the lake again. The seiche can raise the level of the river by 12 to 16 inches.

AMERICAN ROBIN

THE BOYS TAKE THE DOG with them. While not much good at actually catching the birds, she is always first to spot them perching in the trees or hopping about on the grass looking for food.

They take the dog. They take an empty sack to carry the dead birds home, and another bag with bread, cheese, and a bit of dried meat for lunch. They eat lunch under the trees in

the shade by the creek. The burble of the creek is like conversation, and so they don't feel the need to talk. They know each other so well that there is nothing to say anyway.

The boys are brothers — one older, one younger. The older one carries the gun. The younger one carries the sack with the bodies of the robins in it. Sometimes he imagines that the birds are still alive and he has to stop and untie the neck of the sack to look inside and make sure. Sometimes he wants the birds to still be alive so that he could let them go.

The dog points the birds. The older boy shoots them. The younger boy picks them up off the ground and puts them into the sack. That is the arrangement they have, and most days it works well. Most days there is lunch by the creek and 20 or 30 robins in the cloth bag to carry home for supper. This is what they live on — birds, rabbits, squirrels. In the autumn, when there are no leaves on the trees, the boy's father will take them hunting for deer and moose. But now, in the good weather, their father is up north at a lumber camp, working and sending money back to his family. For now it is the two boys who are responsible for feeding their mother and three baby sisters.

The large birds are easier to kill — pigeons, doves, robins, crows. They are easier to kill and there is more meat on their bodies. But there are a lot of settlers shooting birds these days and the passenger pigeon numbers are down, so the boys try mainly for robins because the red breast of the bird makes them easy to see. Also, the dog seems to have a liking for this bird above the others and wants to hunt it.

The younger boy is younger than both his brother and the dog, and he accepts that both of them know better than he does, although most days he prefers the dog because the dog doesn't yell at him when he stops to look inside the sack and make sure that the robins are still dead.

Sometimes at lunch they will lay the dead robins out on the streambank in order of size — a row of red, feathered bricks following the curve of the water. The boys like to look at them while they eat their lunch, like to consider the differences in the birds, and the sameness.

Mostly the laying out of the robins happens when the older boy is in good humour. Today he sits with his arms wrapped around his knees, staring out at the bend in the creek and the younger boy doesn't dare open the sack to remove the birds, even though he wants to.

Instead he chews on the dry heel of bread and thinks about how, after lunch, they will trudge uphill in search of more robins, when what he really wants is to lie down here, in the cool of the creek trees, on the soft grass by the water's edge. He would like to fan the birds out on the bank and lie down beside them.

The boy doesn't mind the killing, but he doesn't like death. He would like to lie down beside the dead robins and keep them company, keep watch for them, the way the dog will keep watch for him while he sleeps at night.

Before he goes to sleep at night he often thinks of the story his mother told him of the robin. She tries to tell him stories about all the animals they kill and eat, and he is not sure if he likes this or not, although he often thinks hard about the stories long after she has told them to him.

The robin, said his mother, has a red breast because he soaked up the blood of Jesus while Jesus hung dying on the cross. The robin sang a song to comfort Jesus while he was dying. He sang into his ear, and the blood from the crown of thorns dripped down from Jesus's head and soaked into the feathers of the bird.

The robin is made of death, thinks the boy, but it does not stop him from wanting to free the bird somehow from death, and while his brother makes circles in the dirt with a stick, and the dog flops in the shade and closes her eyes, the younger boy undoes the neck of the cloth sack and puts his hand inside to offer comfort to the birds.

GREAT BLUE HERON

1.

THEY ARE so easy to kill. He can simply stand under their nests and fire on the adult birds as they glide in to feed their young. And it is so easy to find the nests. All he has to do is work out from a water source, from a creek or river, back to the tall trees at the edge of the marshlands, and there will often be hundreds of nests in one heronry. Each year the birds return to use the same nests, rebuilding and adding to the twig structures, so that some of the older nests are enormous, look big enough for humans. All he has to do is to stand there, in plain sight under these nests, and shoot the birds. Herons are such slow-moving creatures that it is infinitely easier than hunting ducks. It really takes no effort at all, and for each good, long heron feather he will be paid 25 cents — very decent money for 1889.

He has already shot 20 birds this morning. Ten nests of fledgling herons are without parents. But it does not concern him that the baby birds will die of starvation with no adult to feed them. It does not concern him that, after he has plucked the dead adult birds for their feathers, that he will just leave the carcasses to rot in the sun. No, he is only concerned with doing the job that will enable him to get paid. Being a plume hunter requires intense concentration on the task at hand, and little regard for anything else.

But it is the middle of June and the sun is almost overhead and he hasn't been wearing a hat and is hot from standing out all morning in the heat. So he beats back through the marsh grasses to the creek to get a drink. He crouches by the edge, filling his cupped hands with the cool water, and then splashing it over his face and neck. It is only when he straightens up that he sees the heron. It is on the opposite side of the creek, a little ways down from where he has been drinking, and it is standing, very still, in the water by a clutch of bulrushes. It is staring intently into the shallows, hunting, and in its focus and task, the man recognizes himself. He has left his gun leaning up against a tree on the bank of the creek, but he doesn't go for it. If he shoots the heron in the creek, the dead bird will topple into the water and the feathers will get wet and might be spoiled because of that. So, for now, this heron is spared.

The plume hunter has tried not to think of the lives of the birds because he is only concerned with their death. But seeing this heron standing so patiently in the water causes the hunter to feel a flicker of empathy for it.

Before he was a plume hunter, the man worked felling trees. This was harder physical work, and much more dangerous. There is something so peaceful about standing under the living trees at the edge of the marsh, watching the herons swoop down towards their nests, their six-foot wingspans being larger than he is. There is something in their flight that releases something in him, and he is able to tamp that feeling down when he fires on, and kills, the bird, but here, at the creek, seeing the heron fishing, the feeling rises in him again. It is a feeling that belonged to his childhood, and which he was certain he had left behind, so it is astonishing to him now to be watching the heron go about its business of being a heron, and to be filled with wonder at the sight.

Emily Williamson is nervous. The meeting was her idea, and so the burden of it being a success or failure feels to be hers as well. She hurries through the streets towards the teashop, so preoccupied that she forgets to do her usual count. When she pushes open the door and the bell rings, she feels as jangly as the wild rocking of the clapper inside the hull of that bell.

The teashop is filled with women such as herself — women of middle years who have husbands and money, who take long holidays abroad to the continent, and have country houses with staff. How will she know who Mrs. Phillips is?

But then she remembers her count and looks at the tables of women until she sees, in the back corner of the shop, the only hatless woman in the room.

Mrs. Phillips offers her hand. "Four grebes, two herons, and a kittiwake in this room alone," she says, as though reading Emily's thoughts. "The seabird protection league has done nothing at all for the grebe."

Emily Williamson sits down. "We can do better," she says. "Do you not think that we can do better?"

Mrs. Phillips pours the tea. "With our combined memberships, I do think that we can. Not stop the fashion, but let the good women of London know that those feathers in their hats do not come without cost."

"Oh, I am so glad." But what Emily Williamson really feels is relief. She had taken a chance in writing to Mrs. Phillips, in proposing that they merge Mrs. Phillips's Fur and Feathers League with her own Plumage League, in an effort to stop the slaughter of the birds. It was a chance because she knows how people like to keep to their own patch, how they feel that their cause is really the only true cause, and that her offer could have just as easily been taken as an insult.

"We will need a new name, I think," she says, tentatively. But she has nothing to fear from Mrs. Phillips, who seems, reassuringly, to be already two steps ahead of her.

"The Royal Society for the Protection of Birds," says Mrs. Phillips. "Our members will not be allowed to wear, or buy, any hats with feathers, and they must devote themselves to the cause of protecting the birds and discouraging their wanton destruction."

"Oh, very good," says Emily. "Should we order a plate of cakes to celebrate?"

Outside, in the spring sunshine, they walk together down the high street. Emily feels jubilant and tries not to upset this feeling by looking at all the women strolling past with their feathered hats.

"You know what I would like," she says.

"What?"

"To see a great blue heron."

"You'd have to go to the colonies for that," says Mrs. Phillips.

"Yes, I suppose I would."

They walk through the square, the flowering trees already in blossom, the smell of earth and rain rising from the ground.

Mrs. Phillips stops suddenly on the path, turns towards Emily, and stands very stiffly on one leg, the other raised behind her. "They fish like this," she says. "Motionless. For hours." Her strange, statue-like posture in the middle of the square is causing the people around them to regard them curiously, but Mrs. Phillips doesn't shift from her pose.

Emily Williamson never thought she would find commitment so liberating, that her conviction to her cause could promote such happiness within her. She stands in the London sunshine, watching Mrs. Phillips model as a heron, and she feels nothing but gratitude and wonder at the beauty of life.

PLAINSONG

THERE IS COMFORT in thinking that the river is old, and that it will continue after I am dead. This is the appeal of rivers, that they have motion and yet are timeless, allied to our human existence and also alien to it.

Sometimes the river and the land around the river aren't hospitable. Inhospitable is an apt description for the four snakes basking in the sun on the rock, blocking access to the river (one of the snakes bit my dog before the day was out), and for the fact that I sliced my finger on a rock when planting a tree, and for the crazy proliferation of mosquitos who ate me alive while doing that planting. Once a huge, prehistoric-looking snapping turtle crawled out of the river and ambled across the lawn.

It feels like the river is inhospitable when it cuts me, or when the leech waits on the swimming rock, or when the giant snapping turtle crawls out of the river, or when there are masses of snakes writhing at the water's edge. It seems then that the river sends up its creatures to keep other creatures away. I try not to take it personally, but I always notice when it is easy to be near the river, and when it is not.

I often do battle with the beavers on the river. All my trees are wrapped in corsets of chicken wire. Periodically the beavers attempt to build a dam on our little stretch of water and I have to wade into the river to take it apart. Once, in the middle of November, the beavers tried to construct a dam across the opening of the culvert that moves the river under the road at the bottom of my property. I had to wade into the freezing cold water to pull the dam apart. I fell and cut my hand on some rocks, but the water was so cold that my hand didn't bleed until I was out of the river.

Once, I saw a dead beaver, bloated and floating down-stream, with its paws folded solemnly over its chest like an elder statesman.

BEAVER

HUDSON'S BAY
COMPANY
STANDARD
OF TRADE,
1706

1 green three point blanket 2 beavers

1 plain 2 point blanket 1 beaver

6 dozen metal buttons ½ beaver

1 wool hat 1 beaver

1 yard (0.9 metre) blue fabric ¾ beaver

2 yards (1.8 metre) red fabric ¾ beaver

1 file ¼ beaver

1 mirror ⅓ beaver

1 gun 4 beavers

2 dozen (24) flints 1 beaver

2 dozen (24) fish hooks 1 beaver

40 loads of powder and shot 1 beaver

1 powder horn ½ beaver

1 tin pot 1 beaver

1 knife ¼ beaver

5 dozen darning needles (60) ½ beaver

5 dozen (60) brass rings ½ beaver

1 striped cotton shirt ½ beaver

3 (1.4 kg) lbs. soap ½ beaver

1 dozen (12) brass thimbles ¼ beaver

1 pair trousers 1 beaver

1 lb. (0.46 kg) vermilion 4 beavers

1 lb. (0.46 kg) brass wire 1 beaver

Value of Furs:

1 large beaver for 1 beaver

2 small beavers for 1 beaver

2 fox for 1 beaver

10 raccoon for 1 beaver

2 lynx for 1 beaver

5 marten for 1 beaver

4 wolverine for 1 beaver

15 mink for 1 beaver

15 muskrat for 1 beaver

2 land otter for 1 beaver

4 wolf for 1 beaver

3 bear for 1 beaver

There are things that attract us to the river and things that repel us from it, and in any given moment any number of attractions and repellants can be operating. Some days the repellants outnumber the attractions, and some days this is opposite. But it should never be taken personally, because it has nothing to do with our human world; or only insofar as it makes us desire to be near the river, or distant from it.

The river is not welcoming or accepting of us. Some days it doesn't put up a fight, that is all, and that shouldn't be mistaken for benevolence or be given human emotion. It doesn't feel what we do. It doesn't care for us at all. Sometimes the gatekeepers are busy elsewhere and it allows us in, but that doesn't mean that it likes us.

At a friend's place, farther upriver, I found a deer kill one spring. The deer had been trapped by the rocks at the river's edge and couldn't run into the forest, or easily cross the swollen river. The river was an aid to the predator who killed the deer. In this random opportunism, which is such a large part of animal existence, the river can be friend or foe to the creatures that live within and alongside it.

When I haven't been at the cottage for a while, other creatures make use of it. When I arrived last time, blackbirds were perching on all the lawn furniture. Human presence is a barrier that keeps the wildlife a certain distance away, but when we're not around, the wildlife is happy to occupy our spaces and objects, and is reluctant to leave them.

The British naturalist and writer Roger Deakin once said that watching a river is the same as watching a fire in the hearth. Both are moving and alive, and the feeling from watching them is a similar one.

There's a heat wave this week and the cows from the field across the river come down to stand in the river. They have made a path along the riverbank, through the trees, and they stand up to their armpits in the water, bawling — their cries sound like agony, but perhaps it's pleasure — maybe animals make the same noise (animals who could be prey) whether they're happy or unhappy.

It is strange swimming in the river and being separated only by a few branches of willow from the huge black and white cows. I can see the flash of their flanks, rising like walls from the water, and the sweep of their tails as they flick away the deerflies.

A lot of the river smell is decay, rotting plant life especially
— not unpleasant, or particularly strong, but noticeable.
It scents the water, which is only a breath away when I'm
swimming in the river.

It seems that the rotting vegetation smell in the river is
also because of the increased temperature of the water, and
the excessive humidity of the air, making the undersides of
leaves and branches and roots all sweat, and this contributes
to the rank scent.

Swimming is a different experience each time I do it.
Sometimes the river is cold because of rain — the temperature changes all the time — so there is no way of knowing
what to expect from the experience. Sometimes leaves and
pollen and feathers will be blown onto the surface and I will
have to swim through them.

Once a blue barrel floated down to me on the river.
It was filled with an oil and gas mixture, probably for a
lawnmower or outboard engine.

Swimming in the river means that you
are eye level with everything being borne
downstream by the current — floating leaves
on the surface, caterpillars, twigs. Sometimes
a snake will bisect the river, moving just in
front of me, its body rippling the water on
either side of it.

There are always dragonflies over the river. This summer there were a lot of scarlet darter dragonflies. Sometimes when I swim in the river near dark they fly near my head and eat the insects that are coming for me. I love to watch them maneuver above me. There's a myth that dragonflies will sew your eyes shut while you sleep, and another that says they are connected to the underworld — that the dragonfly is the ghost of the nymph and the two states (dragonfly and nymph) are so different from one another that the dragonfly fails to recognize its former self at all. This is the distance between the living and the dead.

You can start swimming in early May, although the water is very cold, and you can stop at the end of September, with the same cold water. The test for how to tell if it's too cold for swimming is to plunge your hand into the river and if the bone in your wrist aches, then the water is too cold to enter.

You never know when the last swim of the season is. One day it is simply just too cold to go in, and there's no predicting when that day might come.

IT'S NOT MY IDEA of a good time, but it's a job. A small job, for the weekend of the festival, but I'll have more money at the end of the weekend than I had at the beginning, and that's what counts. Being a college student is a poor business.

The hall is crammed with tables and each table is loaded with shallow trays. The trays are full of water, and submerged in the water are the frog legs, dozens in each tray. It is my

job to take the frog legs from the water, coat them in batter, and throw them into one of the deep fryers that line half the kitchen. Someone scoops the cooked frog legs out of the fryers, and someone else tosses them into cardboard boxes with fries and coleslaw. Each boxed dinner is sold for nine dollars. People eat outside at picnic benches, and afterwards, at the end of the day, those of us in the kitchen will walk around in the woozy light of the midway, gathering up the garbage and dragging the bags round to the front of the community hall to be piled up against the side of the building.

When I was a child, I liked the festival. I liked the excitement it brought to our small town. I liked seeing all the cars lined up outside the fairgrounds with the out-of-state licence plates. I found the cheesy frog merchandise and signs funny.

But every time I plunge my hands into the water and grab hold of the slippery frog flesh, I cannot help but think of the creature that it was, how it sang confidently into the darkness of the riverbank, how it burrowed into mud, or stretched out across a lily pad. Each time I pull the legs out of the tray it feels like I am catching the frog all over again.

At the end of the three festival days, 80,000 frog legs will have been eaten. That's 40,000 frogs. And while the frogs used to be local, now there aren't enough bullfrogs in the area to supply the festival, and the frozen frog legs are imported from Indonesia. Joshua, who sometimes works at the deep fryers, told me that the French, who also like to consume frog legs, have effectively eaten all of their country's frogs.

My hands are cold from the water in the trays. The hall smells of grease and vinegar and sweat. A warm breeze drifts through the hall from the open doors and stirs the green crepe paper chains looping down from the ceiling.

When I was a girl, my grandmother showed me how to catch frogs by lying a red tablecloth on the riverbank. Frogs like the colour red, and I could simply spread out the table-cloth and wait for the frogs to hop up on it.

Now I could unroll an entire red carpet from the riverbank to the main highway, and there would be no frog traffic. It could be that in my lifetime the frogs will disappear completely. We will have eaten all of them.

How to stop something that is in motion? From my physics lectures I know that Newton's first law of motion states that "an object at rest stays at rest and an object in motion stays in motion . . ." It is natural for objects in motion to resist any changes to that motion. This is what momentum is, and it is very hard to stop something that has momentum. For the frog leg festival to come to an end, it will need to meet something of equal and opposite force.

Really, I don't want to be thinking about this. I just want to do my job, earn some money, and head back to school next

them. They are easy for the boys to net, easy to slip into the jars that the girls carry.

She had expected each jar to glow like a lantern with its cargo of fireflies inside, but this is not what happens. The light does not come on when the fireflies are captured, and each jar is a small pool of darkness that the girls hold tightly in their hands.

The children belong to the local 4-H club. Usually they meet indoors, in daylight. Usually they do crafts or play games or learn the names of plants. But tonight is special. The children have been enlisted by the space program at NASA to help further space exploration. All across the country, 4-H clubs are out tonight with nets and jars, intent on catching lightning bugs. Tomorrow the containers of insects will be shipped to the Goddard Space Flight Center in Greenbelt, Maryland, where the luminous chemicals will be extracted from the tails of the dead fireflies and sent into space in the form of beacons that will be used to attract other life forms in the universe.

A firefly emits "cold light," so called because it produces barely any heat, and this "cold light" will have more effect in outer space than light that requires energy to generate it. She

has read the pamphlets that NASA sent to their 4-H club. She
has learnt a lot about the firefly in the past week, and yet, while
her children are excited about the project, it makes her feel a
little sad to sit out here watching the small lights come on and
the small lights go out. Each firefly shedding its own pattern
of light into the darkness. It is not hard to believe that fireflies
are the souls of the dead come back to find us, or that the sharp
start of light speaks to the very briefness of human life, that
her own life will pass as swiftly as this.

Loneliness is most noticeable when it is echoed. In the
daytime, in the suburb where she lives, in this year of 1965,
with these other families around her, it is easy to believe that
each home is a happy one, that every family hums with love
and industry. But out here, at night — each cigarette a star
across the dark field — she knows that each adult is really just
alone, that no one has the courage to go to another's light, and
that all any of them are essentially teaching their children
tonight is to move towards what is alive, and to extinguish it.

WHITE PINE

H E HAS BEEN in the forest for hours. They sent him in after breakfast and he has wandered through the thick tangle of trees, out into long grass clearings, and back again, feet stumbling over the uneven ground, head tilted up to the sky.

He has marked his path with a knife, cutting into the trees he has passed so that he will be able to find his way out again, but even so he feels lost. His clothes stick to his body with sweat. Insects have raised the flesh on his neck into a bleeding, itchy welt. He regrets volunteering for this task.

And then he doesn't.

It feels good to be alone, to be away from the men and the

yelling and the sounds of steel against wood, the constant thud of the axe and the maul. Here there is no one watching him. He wears the cloak of the forest and he is invisible inside it.

All his life he has been on the water. As a boy he climbed the rigging, slid out along the spars to unroll the stiff canvas sails or haul them in to be reefed in a storm. This is dangerous work, but boys are expendable. He has seen as many as four of them blown from the topmast in a gale. But it was never him, and the older he has become, the closer to the deck he has been allowed to go. Now he doesn't venture up the mast at all, works as a carpenter and, when necessary, as the ship's doctor. The logic being that if a man can repair a join in wood, he can repair a join in bone. But he prefers wood, always has. The truth is that, as he gets older, he likes the company of his fellow men less and less. He finds their laughter hollow, their jokes coarse, their manner offensive. They are loud and greedy, and when he can, he takes his evening meal out to the foredeck and sits watching the silver tips of the waves break against the hull, or the slant of the seabirds across the horizon.

He would like to leave the sea, but what would he do on land? He has no family, no one to return to. What would be the point of a change if there was no one to welcome it?

But the life becomes increasingly intolerable, and especially now, when they have sustained damage from a storm and have been holed up for a fortnight, repairing the ship. When they are in motion, hurtling across the ocean, the men's energies are harnessed to this motion, to their destination, where they will offload one cargo and pick up another. But when the men are engaged in patching the hull, when there is not the sea wind in their veins, they are surly, bad-tempered. They fight with one another over nothing, like dogs scrapping over the memory of a bone.

Which brings him to this moment, to this place, to this perfect tree on the edge of a clearing. A white pine, tall and straight, its upper branches brushing the underside of the sky. The perfect tree for a new mast.

He scores an X into the trunk, so that when the axemen come back, they will cut down the right tree.

His job is done. He must go back to the others, but for a

moment he just stands beneath the pine, looking up. White pines make the best masts because they are straight and strong, bending just enough to accommodate the wind, but never enough to snap. And they already have the sea in them. The sound of their boughs in the breeze is the same *shush shush* of water on the shingle.

He puts his hand out and touches the bark. He wishes he could be like this tree, that he could remake himself, in the middle of his life, into something completely different. That he could have a new life that, when standing on the shore of the old life, was entirely impossible to imagine.

LEAF FLIGHT

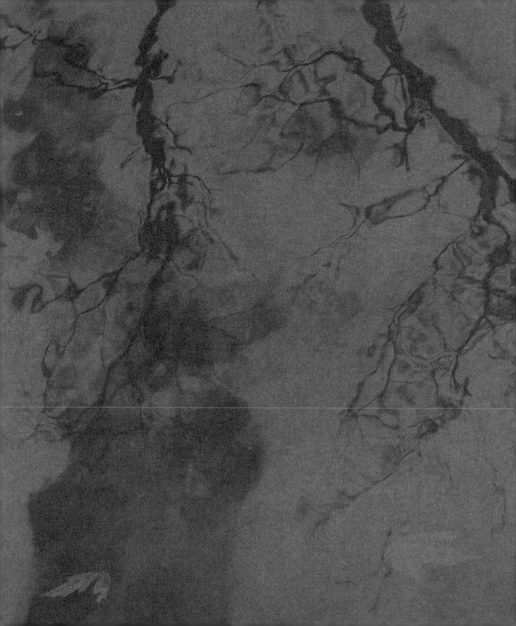

THE RIVER WATER makes gold and silver jewellery shine brighter. After swimming, rings and necklaces sparkle. There is a large vein of white quartz in the rock ledge of the waterfall, and the water must have a high mineral content, because aside from making jewellery gleam, it also makes you feel better for having been immersed in it, as though your skin has been scrubbed and refreshed. It is its own mineral bath and "taking the waters" always feels healing. It is a powerful river and that power is always imminent. And I wonder if this sense of well-being that occurs when you swim in the river, or just sit under the pulse of the waterfall, contributed to it being known by the Chippewa and Algonquin people as a sacred river.

FLORA
ALONG THE
RIVERBANK
FOR
MY PART
OF
DEPOT CREEK

Dogwood

Joe-Pye Weed

Goldenrod

Wild Iris

Common Periwinkle

Swamp Milkweed

Sensitive Fern

Arrowhead

Pickerel Weed

Cattail

Cardinal Flower

White Snakeroot

Yarrow

Jewelweed

ce
ly
,

roghit   Purple Loosestrife

ern   Spotted Joe-Pye Weed

Willow   Turttlehead

Tufted Vetch   Baby's Breath

Swamp Loosestrife   Swamp Vervain

This year and last there have been kingfishers on this pa
of Depot Creek, flying above the winding river in the ea
morning and then again at dusk. There is a large blue here
who likes to fish in the shallows down by the woodshed,
and a hummingbird nest with two hummingbird chicks
on a low branch above the little bay below the waterfall.
There are often turkey vultures overhead, circling out from
the dump grounds which are only about two miles away
by flight but at least ten by road. This summer there was a
redstart in the maple that overhangs the deck, flitting from
branch to branch in a manner that was more butterfly than
bird. Spring brings orioles and finches, blackbirds, robins.
Once, and only once, there was a lawn full of purple martins
when we awoke one late summer morning. And once I saw
a flock of seven mergansers swimming up the river in a very
neat single file. These ducks, like the kingfishers, follow the
winding course of rivers, whether they are flying above
them or swimming in them.

In the autumn there are wild turkeys in the field across the river, bunched up in congress in the grass, or startled into the trees along the riverbank, their heavy bodies teetering on slender branches.

BIRDS
FOUND
ALONG THE
DEPOT CREEK

American Robin

Goldfinch

Redstart

Northern Flicker

Downy Woodpecker

Red-Headed Woodpecker

Belted Kingfisher

Great Blue Heron

Cedar Waxwing

Rose-Breasted Grosbeak

Blue Jay

Crow

Blackbird

Red-Winged Blackbird

Baltimore Oriole

Purple Martin

Turkey Vulture

Red-Tailed Hawk

Wild Turkey

Muscovy Duck

Mallard

Wood Duck

Canada Goose

Ruffed Grouse

Common Merganser

Ruby-Throated
Hummingbird

Eastern Kingbird

Barn Swallow

Barred Owl

Brown Thrasher

I watch a Northern watersnake swallow a fish a third of its size. The snake is resting the top half of its body on a rock shelf at the water's edge, presumably because it would drown if it tried to eat the fish while entirely in the water. The snake is slowly working the muscle of fish down its muscle of gullet, and this requires a certain surrender on the part of the snake, as the task cannot be accomplished quickly. Patience and commitment are necessary and, in this moment of being a terrific predator, the snake is extremely vulnerable because it cannot move when it is in the act of swallowing, and it cannot disgorge the fish to stop the action.

When the fish has been swallowed, the snake doesn't move off right away, but lingers, half on the rocky shore and half in the water. And even though it has just eaten a huge meal, it flicks its tongue to catch the flies that buzz above the surface of the river.

Hunger creates vulnerability. Hunger can be either desire or real physical hunger, but it creates vulnerability in the one who is hungry.

The biggest fish take the deepest part of the pool, leaving the smaller fish around the edges — first to face danger, first to be plucked from the water by predators. The small fish flank the bigger fish. Age takes more protection, commands the safest position, operates from the centre of things.

When the water is shallow, the fish are on the move. Perhaps the coolness of the deep water slows them down and makes them sluggish? Or perhaps the change in activity is motivated by the change in light in the shallow water, a signal of their vulnerability?

The river is a vein or artery for the land, a channel that moves through the body of the earth, that carries away and brings things to the land. What knowledge of the land does it possess? What do the riverbanks think of the river?

The river has pushed its banks many times. Does it have memory of this, or a reach beyond itself that it can feel, that it remembers? What does it feel its true size is? Does the river have a kind of consciousness?

In recent science there is a line of enquiry into "plant neurobiology," which argues that plants display complex behaviours in relationship to various environmental variables and that they are also capable of receiving and transmitting information to other plants. This processing system, while not a brain per se, is a form of intelligence, and a sophisticated one at that. Why would it not also be possible for a complex system such as a river to possess a similar kind of complex intelligence?

Every year something different is dominant within the river ecosystem. The random confluence of weather patterns means that certain species are inclined to prosper during various weather conditions, while others fail.

Last spring and early summer were unusually wet, and the frequent rain made the vegetation along the river more verdant than usual. Things grew at an astonishing rate and there wasn't the usual dieback that there often is at the end of summer, when the parched vegetation shrinks and shrivels. Instead, everything was green and burgeoning, and what surprised me was how quickly the landscape altered because of this. There was bright green algae covering the shelf of granite above the waterfall. Entire rocks along the river's edge became coated in a lush moss and became, in the course of just one season, absolutely unrecognizable as rocks.

Last year the fauna that was having its heyday was snakes. There were snakes everywhere. In other years I often saw a snake or two sunning themselves on the rock shelves near the waterfall, but last summer there were knots of snakes twisting in the grass. A friend came to visit for the afternoon and a snake crawled into the undercarriage of her car, slithering out into her garden when she had arrived home again and parked the car in her driveway.

This year there is a bonanza of chipmunks, which also means that the snake population continues to be a healthy one as they have lots of chipmunks to feed on.

This spring the river receded and left little piles of twigs and mounds of bark in its ebb all along the shore, deposits of what had been kicked up from the bottom in the surge and push of the impressive run-off and flood.

Beavers have stripped bark from a lot of my trees. The river dominates the land and even though I try to shore up trees and shrubs against its force, it enters where it wants and when it wants, and sends out envoys from within its banks — the beavers, snakes, snapping turtles — to colonize or use the land for its own benefit. The land is not separate from the river, but rather the land is controlled by the river, is its proxy, and it is impossible to protect against as it is the stronger force.

In loving the river, I have to acknowledge its indifference not only to me, but to all that I touch and shape on the land that borders it.

The first summer at the property was an unusually warm one, and the river was as hot as bath water. I spent all of my time in the river, hours and hours, days and days. It seems ridiculous to say that it exerted a power over me, but it did feel a little like I was bewitched by it and couldn't stay away. I explored every inch of the riverbed and found many of my treasures that first summer — broken bits of crockery, the child's marble, one of my clay pipes. I got to know my little portion of river so intimately that I know, even now, exactly what is on the bottom in any given spot. There was never another summer as hot as that first one and the river has never warmed up to that degree again, so it has been impossible to spend that same amount of time in it. The randomness of it all sometimes strikes me, and I wonder if a lot of my feeling for the river came about because of that first summer, because I was able to bond with the river so strongly. But that bond was the result of weather conditions, something entirely fickle. What humans like to think is connection is sometimes nothing more than circumstance.

The river is four to five feet lower than it was in the days before the dam. The old riverbanks are hills behind the new riverbanks, which are choked with bog willows and ferns. I have made a garden in one of these hills, in the bend of the river below the waterfall. When I got the property there was a mass of day lilies there, but there must have always been some sort of garden in that spot for the day lilies to have spread so rampantly, and when I cut them back, I discovered a small pink rose bush and a giant white bearded iris. Also, a series of stone steps that climbed from the new riverbank up to the old one.

The problem with making a garden in the old riverbank is that it regularly floods when the spring run-off is high and the river takes back its former borders. This seems to happen at least every second year, sometimes every year. If the flood is for a short duration, everything survives. But if it is for any longer than a week, most of what I have planted in the garden dies. The one plant that doesn't seem to mind being drowned and always bounces back is the bearded iris, which makes me think that it must have been flooded many times in the past, and that perhaps it dates back to the Revelles. A bed of bearded irises can live for 50 years or more.

One summer's day this year I watched a truck park on the edge of the road above the culvert at the bottom of my property. The truck had two big plastic tanks on the back and a man took a large hose down the bank to the river and the truck began to pump water up from the river. When I went to question why they were doing this, the men said that it was perfectly legal and they were taking water for their landscaping company, so that they could water the lawns of the houses they had landscaped. I couldn't believe this would be legal, but when I checked up on it, I found out that they were right. Water conservation laws in Ontario are shockingly lax. It is legal to take up to 50,000 litres a day from any creek or river, pond or lake in Ontario. It does not matter what the size of the body of water is as the law makes no distinction between a large lake, such as Lake Ontario, and a small, shallow stream such as Depot Creek.

50,000 litres is the amount of an average domestic swimming pool. For amounts over 50,000 litres, a permit is required. If the landscaping company that I saw this summer returned every working day for the summer months, they would take over one and a half million litres of water, which is the equivalent of an Olympic-sized swimming pool.

LIST OF FAUNA FOUND ALONG THE DEPOT CREEK

Beaver
Porcupine
Red Fox
Striped Skunk
Fisher
Muskrat
Northern River Otter
Eastern Chipmunk
Red Squirrel
Black Squirrel
Mink
Raccoon
Coyote
Eastern Cottontail Rabbit
Little Brown Bat
White-Tailed Deer
Northern Short-Tailed Shrew

Groundhog
Deer Mouse
American Bullfrog
Green Frog
Northern Leopard Frog
Common Snapping Turtle
Stinkpot
Painted Turtle
Common Gartersnake
Northern Watersnake
Black Rat Snake
Pumpkinseed
Creek Chub
Smallmouth Bass
Perch
Walleye

Grove Snail
Cabbage White Butterfly
Eastern Tiger Swallowtail
Monarch Butterfly
Luna Moth
Mourning Cloak
Spring Azure
Dragonflies and Darters
Firefly
Bumblebees and Honeybees
Yellow Jackets
Harvestmen Spider
Dark Fishing Spider
Banded Garden Spider
Cicada

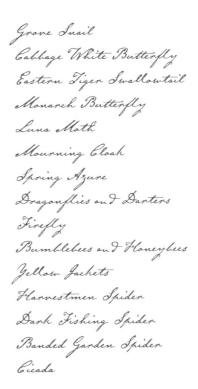

I found an old sepia postcard of the river. The photo is of the Napanee River proper where the river is wide and the current is visible on the surface as ripples. In the photo there are trees massed along the banks and a small footbridge in the distance. The river dominates the photo, and it must have been taken in late summer as the trees are in full bloom and the river is shallow. There is a shoal on the right side of the river and two small ledges of rock in the foreground.

Napanee River, Napanee, Ont.

On the back of the postcard there is a handwritten date
— June 20, 1932 — and below that, first written in pencil
and then traced over in black ink, are the words: "A boy
got drowned in this river yesterday afternoon." The card
is signed "Jean," with a line drawn under the signature.
There is no address filled in, no stamp on the card, so the
postcard was never sent. Perhaps, Jean thought it would be
too disturbing to send a postcard with only the news of a

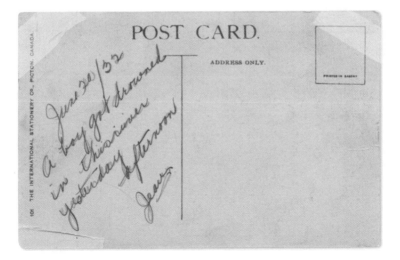

drowning. But it can be assumed that she did initially think of sending it because she so carefully traced over her pencil script with ink. Some time in the tracing of the words and thinking about them again, or looking at the gentle river scene on the front of the postcard and remembering the drowning, Jean changed her mind about sharing the story of the tragedy.

The boy who drowned was Jack ("Jackie") Doolittle, aged seven. According to the local newspaper, he had been playing with his sister, Peggy, in the water at the edge of the river, and he slipped and fell into a "deep hole" that was later revealed to be a whirlpool. He disappeared under the water, and even though a man at the scene dove into the river to try to rescue him, the boy was dead when his body surfaced in shallow water 15 minutes later.

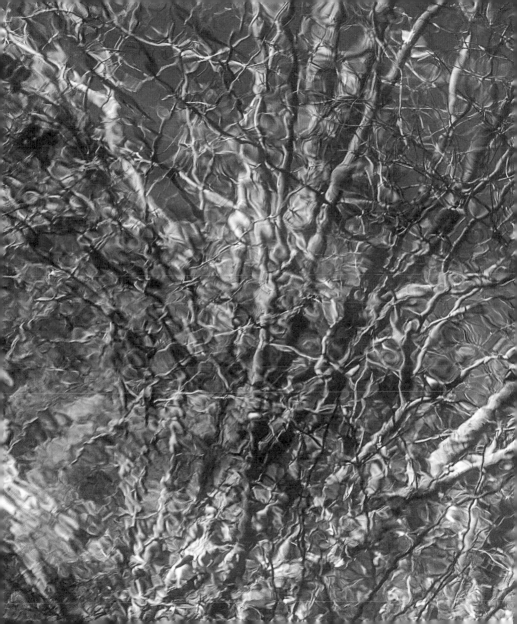

DANDELION

THE LAST OF THE GRASS is stubborn, resists the hoe. I have to kneel and push my hands underneath it, into the earth beneath it, and pry it up. My back hurts from a day of this labour, and I don't lift the last piece of grass up so much as roll it aside. But when that is done and I lurch back to my feet again, I can look out over the lawn of earth that stretches from my boots to the back of my frame house, and I can feel satisfaction at the day's work.

The seeds are in the house, in the dark of the cellar, still in their packets, kept safe and dry between two pieces of burlap. I ordered them in the fall and have kept them through the long winter. I love the hopefulness of the seed catalogue, of thumbing through its cheerful pages at night by candlelight, while the autumn winds strip the last leaves from the trees outside. It was hard to decide what kind of seeds to purchase — French Large-leaved, or American Improved — but in the end I yielded to a twinge of patriotism and chose American Improved. I will not know until this coming autumn whether I have made the correct choice, as my neighbour to the south has decided on French Large-leaved and we will compare our individual harvests.

Twenty years ago settlers brought the plant from Germany, where it was already a famous cure for digestive ailments. It fortifies the blood against illness and can be taken in many forms — as a salad green, or as beer, wine, coffee, or tea. The flower is used for dye. The root is dried and used as an extract. The only part that is unusable is the stem. It truly is the most versatile of plants! And now, in 1870, here in Pennsylvania, almost every second family has taken up their grass lawn to plant the herb. We will plant in the spring, harvest in the fall, and protect the plants through the winter with a covering of muslin, so that there will be many years in which to utilize the plant.

The sun is leaning into the horizon and the light it gives the plot of land at my feet is the rich light of late afternoon, all gold and glory. I imagine that the dandelions will be that light, that I will look through the windows of my house in the mornings and the lawn of yellow flowers will be like the sun fallen to earth, and that sight could only, will only, bring me happiness.

PURPLE LOOSESTRIFE

1870

I WALK THROUGH THE CITY, not by the streets, but by the alley-ways and empty lots, by the railbeds and shoreline. I look down at the ground, never up at the sky to see the changing weather or the position of the sun. I am not interested in the condition of the day, or the sights of New York. What compels my journey through the city is the base materials of the city itself — the sludge and soil that becomes the very ground I walk on. More specifically, it is what grows in that earth that fascinates me, because the plants that struggle up through the tracks of the rails, or out of the dockyard mud, are plants that have never been seen in North America before.

They are what we amateur botanists call "ballast waifs."

Let me explain.

There is a great deal of travel now between Europe and the shores of North America. Not only immigrants make the voyage across the Atlantic, but also livestock and commercial cargo make the crossing. To keep the ships sailing stiffly to windward, it is necessary to have a significant amount of ballast in the hold. This ballast is in the form of moist sand from tidal flats, shovelled aboard before the ships were loaded up, and shovelled out in the North American ports when the ships are unloaded here. Inevitably the sand contains plant seeds from European plants, and the seeds germinate in the hold on the outbound voyage, and then start to grow when they are exposed to sunlight. There are now so many ballast plants that our botanical club has decided to undertake a survey of these plants.

I joined the botanical club because I was interested in meeting other amateur botanists, and in going on the field trips that the club organized around New York City. These weekend field trips, usually to view a rare plant in its natural habitat, were exhilarating to me as I work through the week as a clerk in a bank and none of my fellow clerks know of my hobby. It is such a relief to be in the company of other like minds.

But this survey is much more exciting than a field trip. Here we are, doing something that has never been done before. We are explorers, and I feel, walking through the city, that I am discovering it for the first time.

I have already found a patch of greenpea growing at the edge of the railyard, and the tenacious member of the mustard family, *diplotaxis tenuifolia*, sprouting from between two cracks in the pavement outside the customs house. I have a guide to European plants in one coat pocket, and a notebook and pencil in the other. In my notes I record the location of the plant, its name and condition, and the date that I discovered it. On this, my third weekend participating in the survey, my notebook is already half full.

a   b   c   d   e   f   g

Lythrum Salicaria. 296

I find a clump of petty spurge growing in a back alley, and the rather beautiful zebrina mallow swaying in the afternoon breeze at the base of a garbage heap. I recognize the mallow without the guide because I have been studying the guide on my lunch break from the bank. Although I recognize the plant by sight, I'm less confident in the latin name, so I pull the guide from my pocket and flip through the pages.

I am the son of a brakeman. My job at the bank was thought by my parents to be a betterment to their life, and yet I despise my job. What I had wanted was to become a genuine botanist, to go to school and study, and then to travel to distant lands to unearth new species of plants.

It is strange how sometimes the journey of life is not in what you seek, but what comes to you.

This survey that I am helping to undertake will be published in the bulletin of our botanical club, and it will be used by genuine botanists as a resource. My name will be there, at the top of survey, the first time my name has ever been attached to anything.

Malva sylvestris. I put the plant guide back into my pocket and pull out my notebook.

I admire the ballast waifs. It is no small task to be uprooted and to grow again in new soil, far from home. The desire to thrive is strong, and there is no better evidence of this than in these plants. I would do well to learn from their example.

I make my notes. I continue my walk. At the end of the day I am to meet my fellow amateur botanists and we are to compare our lists. I am as excited about this as I am in taking part in the survey. You see, I am an only child and my parents are dead. I do not have any friends at the bank.

And it is on my way to meet the other club members that I find the most lovely of all the ballast waifs. *Lythrum salicaria*, although I prefer the common name, purple loosestrife. Tall, feathery purple stalks, lining the banks of a small creek that empties into the Hudson.

I have never had a better day than this day. And I know already that this, standing before the stutter of flame that is the purple loosestrife with the sun behind it, is what I will remember of my time here on earth.

WALLEYE

THE ROAD TO THE LAKE is little more than a rutted track and it jostles and bucks the truck, knocking the boy against the door, then into the steering wheel, and then back against the door. Branches clip the windscreen and scrape across the paint. The boy, with difficulty, slows down, remembering the delicate cargo in the bed of the truck. He forgot to adjust the bench seat when he first got in and practically slides under the dash when he presses on the clutch and wrestles the shifter into second gear.

It's not his truck. It's not his job. But his father is ill again, coughing and shaking, unable to rise from his bed, and so the man's tasks fall to the boy and instead of sitting in the hushed calm of the schoolroom, the boy is battling through the wild backcountry on his way to the first of six lakes he will visit before the day is out.

He misses the classroom—the smell of chalk and the quiet scratchings of lead on paper, the feeling of his mind reaching to find an answer or remember an equation. There is a confidence the boy feels in school that he doesn't feel at the wheel of his father's old Ford, but his task is not a difficult one, and he just has to think of this, and to keep the truck bumping along the rutted track.

The first lake appears without warning, a flicker of blue through the thin trees, and then the great wash of it spread out before him as he shudders the truck to a stop in a small clearing by the shore.

There are 36 pails in the back of the Ford, six pails per lake. The boy lowers the tailgate and struggles the first two pails down to the edge of the water. The metal containers are heavy, each one choked full with its cargo of tiny viscous dots, the eyed eggs of the walleye, fresh from the hatchery. He puts the first two pails down on the lick of beach and looks out across the lake. His father said to place the eggs on a shoal, but what is he to do if there is no shoal? The boy feels panic move its cold wave through his body, and he closes his eyes for a moment and thinks of his desk at school and the reassuring sight of his pencils and ruler laid out in straight lines at the top of his exercise book.

There's no shoal, but there is a wider section of beach about a hundred yards to the left, so the boy removes his shoes and wades into the lake with the pails of eggs. The water is warm and the sand feels good against the soles of his feet. He walks slowly through the water, moving towards the large apron of sand by a stand of birch trees.

The eggs are smaller than a pencil eraser, round and pink, with two black specks in each one to show the eyes of the embryonic walleye. The eggs look like miniature eyeballs themselves, and when the boy tips the pails into the water at the edge of the beach, he has to remind himself that the eggs are actually fish and will, with luck, swim out of these shallows in a few weeks and head for the deeper, cooler water, where, in several years, they will be hauled out by the sport fishermen who visit this lake every summer.

The boy does not fish himself. He used to have a friend who he went fishing with, a Native boy whose father was a guide for the hunters who come up from the city in the fall. The guide's son was called Connie, which the boy's father said was a girl's name when he found out about the friendship and put a stop to it. Never mind, Connie said, it's not my real name anyway.

But before that, when they were still friends and went fish-ing, they had caught a trout one afternoon and Connie had made

them put it back, even though it was plenty big enough to eat. But he had explained to the boy that the Great Spirit had once been hungry and caught a trout like this one, but when he saw how beautiful and powerful the fish was, he decided that it should live and that he would go hungry. Connie had flipped the fish over to show the boy the coloured spots on the fish's belly where the fingers of the Great Spirit had once held onto it. The bright spots looked like stars in the night sky.

And now the boy doesn't fish anymore, and Connie has gone, and the boy's father takes to the bottle most nights and now most mornings can't rise from his bed. The boy's mother left long ago because of this, but the boy can't leave yet and all he wants is for his friend to come back, and to get the answer right and have the teacher praise him and lay her cool, gentle hand on his head as she passes by his desk.

The fish eggs aren't fish. One thing is not yet the other. The eggs lie together in the shallow water at the edge of the lake. The boy nudges the small pile with his bare foot. *Swim*, he thinks. *Hurry up and grow big. Hurry up and get away from here.*

ENDINGS

IT IS HARD TO FATHOM the age of the river, to fully imagine how old 170 million years is. When the river was new there were dinosaurs on the earth. There were no birds yet, just flying lizards. The river is older than birds. How to properly imagine what that world was like?

The river has known so much, has carried so much and so many on its back. I sometimes wonder if it simply wants to be left alone to run quietly in its channel, ferrying its cargo of fish and plants and communicating with the riverbed and riverbanks — that anything else is a broach, an intrusion. That everything else is an effort.

And just as there was no way to begin this essay on the river, there is no way to end it. All through the writing of these words the river has been moving, and it will continue to move after I have put down my pen and stood up from my chair. I simply have to step out of this story, as I would step out of the river. And as there were multiple beginnings, so there are multiple endings.

We tell a story for two reasons — to remember it and to forget it — the repeated telling helps solidify experience into a tangible and also takes away its power to hurt us. Repeated retelling numbs our feelings but sharpens our sense of the narrative. Is the river an embodiment of storytelling? The flow of water, the movement, is a way for the river to constantly remember itself and forget itself.

The way the history of Bellrock and the area changes with each piece of information I find is like the river itself. History is a moving, snaking thing that is constantly shifting and altering its landscape depending on who is doing the telling or remembering.

Is the river our snake brain and so we understand it on a primordial level, the level of instinct rather than language?

Does the river produce the same feelings in the succession of human beings who travel on it or swim in it? Did the Chippewa and Algonquin people, paddling Depot Creek at dusk, feel from the river what Russell the frogger felt, or what the legions of river drivers felt, or what I feel when I'm canoeing it?

There's a section of the river, where it first enters the bog and the dead trees stand sentinel in the drowned lands, and fallen trees drip moss and lichen from their mouldering branches, where the river feels very remote and old, dense like the Everglades, and a little frightening.

Did it always feel this way? Is entering the river a kind of time travel, where we are able to briefly glimpse other times and other people from the common experience of being in and on this ancient waterway? Is that how the river communicates with us?

Through all of it — through the various layers of human history and the remembering or forgetting of that past — through the surges of season — the lifespan of vegetation and animals dependent on it — the river just keeps flowing in its channel.

A better way to think about the river's flow is perhaps to measure it with what is on or near it. So, that the flight of a leaf downstream would be counted, not by chronological time, but by the cadence of breaths I take, the wingbeats of a bird overhead, the number of raindrops, the footsteps of the dog, my heartbeats.

It's autumn now, and the grass is soaked with dew in the mornings, as though the river has climbed out of itself and crawled across the lawn. There is mist above the water and for a day or two, perhaps a week if we're lucky, the river water will be warmer than the air, will hold the last of summer in its mouth.

The blackbird sings after every sip of water.

ACKNOWLEDGEMENTS

For their help with the research for this book, I would
like to thank Heather Home at the Queen's University
Archives, Shelley Respondek at the Lennox and Addington
County Archives, Nick Adams for supplying archaeological information, Mary McDonald for her stellar research
on Mrs. Coffey, the staff of the Map Library at Queen's
University, Gary and Heather Kembel.

Portions of this book have been previously published in
the *Queen's Quarterly*.

Pam Roel and Janice Hindley have been
very kind in corresponding with me
about their grandfather, Russell Revelle,
and in sending me photographs of his
tenure on the river. I am exceedingly
grateful for their help.

Tama Baldwin photographed the river in all four seasons and her rigorous intellect and keen eye helped inform this narrative. Her beautiful photographs can be seen at tamabaldwin.com.

Kim Ondaatje has lived alongside Depot Creek for many years and been its devotee. It was a conversation with her that began this book. I thank her for that, and for our many talks about the river.

Joanne Page has been my canoeing companion along Depot Creek and the Napanee River. We had ourselves some excellent adventures, didn't we just.

Thanks to Kelley Aitken for her sketches of the river.

Thanks to Nancy Jo Cullen, as always.

Stan Dragland and Beth Follett celebrated the river often with me. Stan's novel about Depot Creek is *The Drowned Lands*, published by Pedlar Press.

I want to thank Walter Lloyd, Lorrie Jorgensen, Duane and Judy Asselstine for assistance with the river property.

Thank you, Jennifer Ross, for the sublime conversations about rivers.

Thanks to my agent, Clare Alexander, for her support of this project.

And finally, I would like to thank my editor, Susan Renouf, for shaping this book from start to finish. It is always so wonderfully inspiring to work with you.

SELECTED BIBLIOGRAPHY

Adams, Nick. "A Great Collection of Indian Relics from a Destroyed Late Archaic and Early Woodland Mortuary Centre in Eastern Ontario." Paper presented at the 21st Annual Meeting of the Canadian Archaeological Association, Fredericton, 1989.

Carter, Floreen Ellen. *Place Names of Ontario*. London, ON: Phelps, 1984.

Deakin, Roger. *Notes from Walnut Tree Farm*. London: Penguin, 2009.

Edwards, Frank B. *The Smiling Wilderness: An Illustrated History of Lennox and Addington*. Camden, ON: Camden House Publishing, 1984.

Frontenac County. *Enhanced Census of Portland Township*. 1881.

Frontenac County History Committee. *County of a Thousand Lakes: The History of the County of Frontenac 1673–1973*. Kingston: Frontenac County Council, 1982.

Government of Ontario, Department Planning and Development. *Conservation in Eastern Ontario*. 1946.

Government of Ontario, Department Planning and Development. *Conservation in Eastern Ontario*. 1957.

Illustrated Historical Atlas of Frontenac, Lennox and Addington Counties, Ontario. J.H. Meacham & Company, 1878.

Kingston Whig-Standard. October 2, 1935.

Napanee Beaver. July 27, 1932.

Pollan, Michael. "The Intelligent Plant: Scientists Debate a New Way of Understanding Flora." *New Yorker*. December 23 and 30, 2013, 93.

Sliter, Dorothy Murray. *The Friendly Village*. Privately published, 1967.

IMAGE CREDITS

COVER

FRONT: Map © Department of Natural Resources Canada; *Dead robin* © Csaba Peterdi/Dreamstime
.com; *Women on shore, c. 1912* © marlenka/iStockphoto; *Cardinal flower* by Louisa Anne Meredith,
c. 1836. BACK: insect from *Field Book of Insects* by Frank E. Lutz, c. 1918, courtesy Biodiversity
Heritage Library; Hewing felled timber, operations of McFadden & Gillies, Jocko Rivers, Ont.,
W.D. Watt, Booth family album, W.D. Watt/Library and Archives Canada, accession 1979-208
NPC, PA-121799; plant from *American Crow*, plate 156, by John J. Audubon, courtesy audubon.org

INTERIOR

1: Map, see cover credit

4–5: *Verbena hastata*/vervain detail, from the Thomas Fisher Rare Book Library, University of Toronto

6: Bee from *Field Book of Insects*, see cover credit

7: Detail from *Ruby-throated Hummingbird*, plate 47, by John J. Audubon, courtesy audubon.org

15: Found teeth photographed by Nancy Jo Cullen, April 2015

32: Map of Bellrock, from the author's collection

35: Postcard N9428, courtesy Lennox and Addington County Archives

39: Detail from Anna Atkins's cyanotype photogram of *Carix (America)*, c. 1850, in the public domain
    on Google Cultural Institute, from the George Eastman House Collections, purchased with funds
    provided by Ford Motor Co. and from Margaret T. Morris Foundation

49: Photographs of the Revelles courtesy Pam Roel and Janice Hindley

54–55: Various found objects photographed by Nancy Jo Cullen, April 2015

56–57: *Cattails (Scirpus lacustris, Typha latifolia)* courtesy the UBC Botanical Garden Archives, acces-
    sion 2005.680.1598

58: *End view of John's house, Canada*, 1837, by Anne Langton, F 1077-8-1-4-19, Archives of Ontario,
    I0008042

60: *Song Sparrow in the Cattails*, ℗ Ingrid Taylar, April 2013, flickr.com/photos/taylar

62: Cabbage white butterfly photo courtesy CSIRO

63: Ship photo from "In Quarantine: Life and Death on Grosse Îsle, 1832–1937," C-022139, Library
    and Archives Canada

64: Detail from textual record of Subject files of the Offices of the Governor-in-Chief at Quebec, the
    Governor-in-Chief of the Province of Canada and the Governor General of the Dominion of
    Canada, en ligne No. MIKAN 126292 (item 1), Library and Archives Canada

66: Cabbage illustration detail from Botanical Printables

68: *Small Cabbage White Butterfly* by Richard Bartz, a.k.a. Makro Freak, June 2007

71: Cardinal flower illustration detail from *The New Botanic Garden*, c. 1812, courtesy the Biodiversity Heritage Library

72: Portrait of William Bligh painted by J. Ruffell, royal painter to His Majesty and Their Royal Highnesses the Prince of Wales and Duke of York, engraved by J. Condé, c. 1792

73: Detail from Henry Roberts' *The Resolution*, SAFE/PXD 11, No. a156061, courtesy Mitchell Library, State Library of New South Wales

74–75: *Cardinal flower* by Louisa Anne Meredith, c. 1836

77: Cardinal flower (*Lobelia cardinalis*), U.S. Fish and Wildlife Service, Dr. Thomas G. Barnes

81: *Ruby-throated Hummingbird*, plate 47, by John J. Audubon, courtesy audubon.org

93: Joanne Page in a canoe on the Napanee River, from the author's collection

100: Illustration of the river © Kelley Aitken | www.kelleyaitken.ca

102: *American Robin (Turdus migratorius) Eggs in Nest*, by Laslovarga

103: *American Robin* by John J. Audubon, University of Pittsburgh, via Wikimedia Commons

104: *American Robin (Turdus migratorius) Perched on an Apple Tree in Spring* by Arustleund, via Wikimedia Commons

109: Illustration of great blue heron from *Birds That Hunt and Are Hunted: Life Histories of One Hundred and Seventy Birds of Prey, Game Birds and Waterfowls*, Neltje Blanchan, c. 1902, courtesy the Biodiversity Heritage Library

111: *Heron 2*, ⓘ Teresa Shen, December 2012, flickr.com/photos/tshen91

113: *Vanderbilt Cup Auto Race, Mrs. H.P. Whitney in Box*, c. 1908, from George Grantham Bain Collection, Library of Congress

114: Detail of Victorian ladies' summer hats, May 1900 issue of *The Delineator* magazine

120–121: *Beaver Dam*, ⓘⓒⓔ Gerry Dincher, January 2013, flickr.com/photos/gerrydincher

122: Detail from *Le Castor* illustration by De Sere, engraved by Vinkeles, c. 1780, courtesy Library and Archives Canada, Acc. No. R9266-2583

122–123: Background tree image ⓔ StockSnap.io

123: Beaver engraving from an unknown source

126–127: Aerial view of the river photographed by drone in June 2015, Kingston Aerial Photography Ltd. (Kelvin Clark)

134: *Bullfrog Eyes*, ⓘⓒⓔ Nick Harris, May 2010, flickr.com/photos/nickharris1

137: Detail from *Helleborena, The Lady's Slipper of Pennsylvania*, with bullfrog (*Rana maxima*) illustration by Mark Catesby, c. 1722, courtesy Swallowtail Garden Seeds

138: *Bullfrog (Rana catesbeiana)*, ⓘⓒⓔ Joshua Mayer, May 2010, flickr.com/photos/wackybadger

140: Firefly © Radim Schreiber | www.FireflyExperience.org